T0341786

the message of

2 TIMOTHY

Series editors:
Alec Motyer (OT)
John Stott (NT)
Derek Tidball (Bible Themes)

the message of

2 TIMOTHY

Guard the gospel
Revised edition

John Stott

INTER-VARSITY PRESS
36 Causton Street, London SW1P 4ST, England
Email: ivp@ivpbooks.com
Website: www.ivpbooks.com

Originally published under the title Guard the Gospel *in 1973*
First published as The Message of 2 Timothy *in 1984*
Reprinted nine times
New edition (with study guide) 1999
Reprinted 2000, 2002, 2005 (twice), 2007, 2009, 2010, 2012
This edition published 2021

British Library Cataloguing-in-Publication Data
A catalogue record for this book is available from the British Library

ISBN: 978–1–78974–243–5
eBook ISBN: 978–1–78359–070–4

Set in 9.5/13pt Karmina
Typeset in Great Britain by CRB Associates, Potterhanworth, Lincolnshire

Produced on paper from sustainable forests.

*Inter-Varsity Press publishes Christian books that are true to the Bible
and that communicate the gospel, develop discipleship and strengthen the church
for its mission in the world.*

*IVP originated within the Inter-Varsity Fellowship, now the Universities and Colleges
Christian Fellowship, a student movement connecting Christian Unions in universities
and colleges throughout Great Britain, and a member movement of the International
Fellowship of Evangelical Students. Website: www.uccf.org.uk. That historic association
is maintained, and all senior IVP staff and committee members subscribe
to the UCCF Basis of Faith.*

Contents

Bible Speaks today

GENERAL PREFACE

The Bible Speaks Today describes three series of expositions, based on the books of the Old and New Testaments, and on Bible themes that run through the whole of Scripture. Each series is characterized by a threefold ideal:

- to expound the biblical text with accuracy
- to relate it to contemporary life, and
- to be readable.

These books are, therefore, not 'commentaries', for the commentary seeks rather to elucidate the text than to apply it, and tends to be a work rather of reference than of literature. Nor, on the other hand, do they contain the kinds of 'sermons' that attempt to be contemporary and readable without taking Scripture seriously enough. The contributors to The Bible Speaks Today series are all united in their convictions that God still speaks through what he has spoken, and that nothing is more necessary for the life, health and growth of Christians than that they should hear what the Spirit is saying to them through his ancient – yet ever modern – Word.

ALEC MOTYER
JOHN STOTT
DEREK TIDBALL
Series editors

Author's preface

During the gestation of this book I seem to have lived inside this second letter of Paul to Timothy. In imagination I have sat down beside Timothy and have tried myself to hear and heed this final charge from the ageing apostle. I have also tried to share its message with many people: with the congregation of All Souls Church, Langham Place, in the autumn of 1967; with about nine thousand students at the great Urbana missionary conference in the USA in December 1967; with those attending the 1969 Keswick Convention; with groups of pastors at various times in America, Wales, Ireland, New Zealand, Australia and Singapore; and with some Anglican bishops before the 1968 Lambeth Conference. On each occasion I have been impressed afresh by the timeliness for today of what the apostle writes, especially for young Christian leaders. For our era too is one of theological and moral confusion, even of apostasy. And the apostle summons us, as he summoned Timothy, to be strong, brave and steadfast.

The words which crystallize the letter for me are the two little mono-syllables *sy de* ('but as for you'), which occur four times. Timothy is called to be different. He is not to yield to the pressures of public opinion or conform to the spirit of his age, but rather to stand firm in the truth and the righteousness of God. In my judgment nothing is more needed by Christians in today's world and church than this same courage.

I express my warm gratitude to my secretary, Frances Whitehead, for her efficient and tireless labours during the past seventeen years, not least in the typing of innumerable manuscripts. She is not likely to forget this one, since it was the indirect cause of an accident which involved her in the pain of a dislocated toe!

JOHN STOTT

Chief abbreviations

AG   *A Greek–English Lexicon of the New Testament and Other Early Christian Literature* by William F. Arndt and F. Wilbur Gingrich (University of Chicago Press and Cambridge University Press, 1957).

Alford   *The Greek Testament: A Critical and Exegetical Commentary* by Henry Alford. Vol. 3 (Rivingtons, fourth edition, 1865).

AV   The Authorized (King James) Version of the Bible, 1611.

Barrett   *The Pastoral Epistles* by C. K. Barrett (The New Clarendon Bible, Oxford University Press, 1963).

Calvin   *The Epistles of Paul to Timothy and Titus* by John Calvin, 1548 (Oliver and Boyd, 1964).

Ellicott   *The Pastoral Epistles of St. Paul* by C. J. Ellicott, 1861 (Longmans, fourth edition, 1869).

Eusebius   *The Ecclesiastical History* by Eusebius, Bishop of Caesarea, 4th century AD. Translated by H. J. Lawlor and J. E. L. Oulton (SPCK, 1927).

Fairbairn   *Commentary on the Pastoral Epistles* by Patrick Fairbairn, 1874 (Oliphants and Zondervan, 1956).

Guthrie   *The Pastoral Epistles* by Donald Guthrie (Tyndale New Testament Commentaries, Tyndale Press and Eerdmans, 1957).

Hanson   *The Pastoral Letters* by A. T. Hanson (The Cambridge Bible Commentary on the New English Bible, Cambridge University Press, 1966).

Hendriksen   *The Epistles to Timothy and Titus* by William Hendriksen (Baker Book House, 1957, and Banner of Truth Trust, 1959).

JB	The Jerusalem Bible (Darton, Longman and Todd, 1966).
JBP	*The New Testament in Modern English* by J. B. Phillips (Collins, 1958).
Lock	*The Pastoral Epistles: A Critical and Exegetical Commentary* by Walter Lock (The International Critical Commentary, T. and T. Clark, 1924).
LS	*Greek–English Lexicon* compiled by H. G. Liddell and R. Scott. New edition by H. S. Jones (Oxford University Press, 1925–40).
MM	*The Vocabulary of the Greek Testament* by J. H. Moulton and G. Milligan, 1930 (Hodder and Stoughton, 1949).
Moule	*The Second Epistle to Timothy* by Handley C. G. Moule (The Devotional Commentary series, Religious Tract Society, 1905).
NEB	The New English Bible (New Testament, 1961; Old Testament, 1970).
NIV	The New International Version of the Bible (1973, 1978, 1984, 2011).
Plummer	*The Pastoral Epistles* by Alfred Plummer (The Expositor's Bible, Hodder and Stoughton, 1888).
RSV	The Revised Standard Version of the Bible (New Testament, 1946; Old Testament, 1952; revised edition, 1971).
Simpson	*The Pastoral Epistles* by E. K. Simpson (Tyndale Press, 1954).
White	*The Pastoral Epistles* by Newport J. D. White (The Expositor's Greek Testament, Hodder and Stoughton, 1910).

Introduction

Bishop Handley Moule confessed that he found it difficult to read Paul's second letter to Timothy 'without finding something like a mist gathering in the eyes'.[1] Understandably so. It is a very moving human document.

We are to imagine the apostle, 'Paul the old man', languishing in some dark, dank dungeon in Rome, from which there is to be no escape but death. His own apostolic labours are over. 'I have finished the race,' he can say. But now he must make provision for the faith after he has gone, and especially for its transmission (uncontaminated, unalloyed) to future generations. So he sends Timothy this most solemn charge. He is to preserve what he has received, at whatever cost, and to hand it on to faithful people who in their turn will be able to teach others also (2:2).

In order to grasp the letter's message and feel its full impact, it is necessary to understand the background against which it was written. Four points need to be made.

1. This is a genuine letter of Paul to Timothy

The genuineness of the three pastoral epistles was almost universally accepted in the early church. References to them occur possibly in the Corinthian letter of Clement of Rome as early as *c.* AD 95, probably in the letters of Ignatius and Polycarp during the first decades of the second century, and certainly in the works of Irenaeus towards the end of the century. The Muratorian Canon, which dates from about AD 200, ascribes all three letters to the apostle Paul. The only exception to this testimony is the heretic Marcion who was excommunicated in AD 144 in

---

[1] Moule, p. 16.

Rome. But he had theological reasons for rejecting these (and other) New Testament letters, and Tertullian expressed surprise that he had omitted the Pastorals from his canon. Eusebius in the fourth century included them among 'the fourteen epistles of Paul' which 'are manifest and clear (as regards their genuineness)', the fourteenth being the epistle to the Hebrews which (he added) some rejected as not Pauline.[2]

This external witness to the authenticity of the pastoral epistles continued as an unbroken tradition until in 1807 F. Schleiermacher rejected 1 Timothy, and in 1835 F. C. Baur spurned 2 Timothy and Titus as well. Since then scholars have ranged themselves on each side of the debate, and the Pastorals have had both powerful critics and spirited champions. For a detailed critique the reader is referred to P. N. Harrison's *The Problem of the Pastorals* (1921), and for a careful defence of the traditional Pauline authorship to the commentaries by William Hendriksen (pp. 4–33) and Donald Guthrie (pp. 12–52 and 212–228). The issues can only be sketched here.

The right place to begin is to recognize that in the first verse of each of the three letters the writer gives a clear and solemn claim to be the apostle Paul. He goes on to refer to his former persecuting zeal (1 Tim. 1:12–17), to his conversion and commission as an apostle (1 Tim. 1:11; 2:7; 2 Tim. 1:11) and to his sufferings for Christ (e.g. 2 Tim. 1:12; 2:9, 10; 3:10, 11). More than that, the personality of the apostle seems to permeate these letters. Handley Moule wrote of 2 Timothy: '*The human heart* is in it everywhere. And fabricators, certainly of that age, did not well understand the human heart.'[3] Hence even those who deny the Pauline authorship of these letters tend to believe that the writer has incorporated genuine Pauline fragments in his work.

The first reason the Pauline authorship of the Pastorals is questioned is *historical*. It is argued that since they mention visits by Paul to Ephesus and Macedonia (1 Tim. 1:3), Crete and Nicopolis (Titus 1:5; 3:12), Troas, Miletus and Rome (2 Tim. 1:17; 4:13, 20) which cannot be reconciled with Luke's record in Acts of the apostle's journeys, these must therefore be the author's fabrication or at best genuine visits which he has ingeniously misplaced. But if the apostle was released from his Roman imprisonment and then resumed his travels (as he expected and tradition says), before

---

[2] Eusebius, 111.3.5.

[3] Moule, p. 21.

being re-arrested, it is perfectly possible to reconstruct the order of events (as we shall soon see) without any need to accuse the author of fiction or romance.

The second argument is *literary*. Critics reject the Pauline authorship of the Pastorals on the ground that much of their vocabulary is absent from the other ten letters attributed to Paul (and some from the whole New Testament), while many characteristic Pauline expressions in those ten letters are absent from the Pastorals. There are plenty of 'Paulinisms' in the Pastorals, however, both of style and of language, and the changes of time, situation and subject matter are sufficient to account for the peculiarities. 'Great souls are not their own mimes,' as E. K. Simpson justly comments.[4]

The third and *theological* argument takes various forms. Some claim that the God of the earlier Pauline letters (Father, Son and Holy Spirit) and the grace-faith-salvation-works syndrome have become subtly changed and no longer ring true. But there can be no doubt that the Pastorals set forth the electing, redeeming initiative of 'God our Saviour' who has given his Son to die as our ransom and to rise again, and who now justifies us by his grace and regenerates us by his Spirit, in order that we may live a new life of good works. Others urge that the prevalent heresy which lies behind the Pastorals – its denial of the resurrection, its love of asceticism, its 'myths' and its 'genealogies' – is the developed Gnosticism of the second century, perhaps of Marcion himself. This supposition ignores, however, the *Jewish* aspects of the heresy (e.g. Titus 1:10, 14; 3:9; 1 Tim. 1:3–11) and its evident similarities to the Colossian heresy to which the apostle has already addressed himself a year or two previously.

The fourth argument is *ecclesiastical*, namely that the church structures found in the Pastorals are those of the second century, including the monarchical episcopate to which Bishop Ignatius of Antioch referred in his letters. Some critics go further and find the whole atmosphere of the Pastorals too 'churchy' for Paul. Ernst Käsemann[5] quotes Martin Dibelius as having once said that the pastoral epistles 'mark the beginning of the bourgeois outlook in the church'. He adds that he cannot himself regard as Pauline letters in which the church has become 'the central theme of theology', 'the gospel is domesticated' and Paul's image is 'heavily daubed

---

[4] Simpson, p. 15.
[5] *Jesus Means Freedom* (SCM, 1969), p. 88.

by church piety'.[6] We can only reply that this is an extremely subjective judgment. Paul's earliest letters already give evidence of a high doctrine of the church and the ministry, and Luke tells us that it was his policy to ordain elders in every church from his first missionary journey onwards (Acts 14:23). That he should have developed this further in the Pastorals, with instructions about the selection and appointment of ministers, the worship of the church and the maintenance of doctrine, is entirely understandable. But the church and ministry he describes are still recognizably the same, and there is no monarchical episcopate or threefold ministry yet, because 'bishops' and 'elders' are still the same order.

Consequently, the conclusion of many scholars is still that the arguments which have been advanced to deny the Pauline authorship of the pastoral epistles – historical, literary, theological and ecclesiastical – are not sufficient to overthrow the evidence, both external and internal, which authenticates them as genuine letters addressed by the apostle Paul to Timothy and Titus.

2. The Paul who wrote it was a prisoner in Rome

He describes himself as our Lord's 'prisoner' (1:8), and this was his second Roman imprisonment. He was not now enjoying the comparative freedom and comfort of his own hired house, in which Luke takes leave of him at the end of Acts and from which he seems to have been set free, as he expected. Instead, he was incarcerated in some 'dismal underground dungeon with a hole in the ceiling for light and air'.[7] Perhaps it was the Mamertine prison, as tradition says. But wherever he was, Onesiphorus succeeded in finding him only after a painstaking search (1:17). He was certainly in chains (1:16), 'chained like a criminal' (2:9). He was also suffering acutely from the loneliness, the boredom and the cold of prison life (4:9–13). The preliminary hearing of his case had already taken place (4:16–17). Now he was awaiting the full trial, but was not expecting to be acquitted. Death appeared to him inevitable (4:6–8). How had this come about?

It seems that, after being released from his earlier imprisonment (the house arrest in Rome described at the end of Acts), Paul 'again journeyed

---

6 *Jesus Means Freedom*, pp. 89, 97.

7 Hendriksen, p. 234.

on the ministry of preaching'.[8] He went to Crete where he left Titus behind (Titus 1:5), and then to Ephesus where he left Timothy behind (1 Tim. 1:3–4). He may well have gone on to Colossae to see Philemon, as he had planned (Phlm. 22), and he certainly reached Macedonia (1 Tim. 1:3). Of the Macedonian cities he visited, one will have been Philippi (Phil. 2:24). From Macedonia he addressed his first letter to Timothy in Ephesus and his letter to Titus in Crete. He told Titus his intention to spend the winter at Nicopolis (Titus 3:12), a town in Epirus on the west (Adriatic) coast of Greece. Presumably he did this, and presumably, as he requested, Titus joined him there. If the apostle was ever able to fulfil his great ambition to evangelize Spain (Rom. 15:24, 28), it must have been in the following spring that he set sail. Clement of Rome in his famous letter to the Corinthians (chapter 5) said that Paul had 'come to the extreme limit of the west'. He may have been referring only to Italy, but a reference to Gaul or Spain – and even Britain (as some have suggested) – seems more likely.

It is safe to assume that he later kept his promise to revisit Timothy in Ephesus (1 Tim. 3:14–15). From there his itinerary seems to have taken him to the nearby port of Miletus, where he had to leave Trophimus behind ill (2 Tim. 4:20), to Troas (the port from which he had first set sail for Europe), where he stayed with Carpus and left his cloak and some books behind (2 Tim. 4:13), to Corinth, where Erastus left the party (2 Tim. 4:20; cf. Rom. 16:23), and so to Rome. Somewhere on this journey he must have been re-arrested. Was it at Troas, explaining why he had no opportunity to collect his personal belongings together but had to leave them behind in Carpus's house? Or was it only when he reached Rome? We do not know the circumstances. But we do know that he was again arrested and again imprisoned, that this time he had to endure great hardship, and that there was to be no escape. For the Neronian persecution was in full swing (AD 64). And the tradition is likely to be correct that Paul was condemned to death and then beheaded (as a Roman citizen would have been) on the Ostian Way about 3 miles outside the city. Eusebius quotes Dionysius of Corinth that Paul and Peter 'were martyred both on the same occasion', though he adds that Paul's execution was by beheading and Peter's (at his own request) by crucifixion 'head-downwards'.[9]

---

[8] Eusebius, 11.22.2.

[9] Eusebius, 11.25.5, 8 and 111.1.2.

Shortly before he died, during his further and more severe imprisonment, Paul sent this second message to Timothy. His execution seemed to him imminent, so that he was writing under its shadow. Although it was an intensely personal communication to his young friend Timothy, it was also – and consciously – his last will and testament to the church.

3. The Timothy to whom the letter was addressed was being thrust into a position of responsible Christian leadership far beyond his natural capacity

For over fifteen years, since he had first been recruited in his home town Lystra, Timothy had been Paul's faithful missionary companion. He had travelled with him throughout most of the second and third missionary journeys and had been sent during them as a trusted apostolic delegate on several special missions, such as to Thessalonica and Corinth (1 Thess. 3:1ff.; 1 Cor. 4:17). He had then accompanied Paul to Jerusalem (Acts 20:1–5) and may have been with him on the perilous voyage to Rome. At all events, he was certainly in Rome during the first imprisonment, for the apostle bracketed Timothy's name with his own when he wrote the prison epistles to Philemon, the Philippians and the Colossians (Phlm. 1; Phil. 1:1; 2:19–24; Col. 1:1).

It is not just that Paul had a strong affection for Timothy as a friend whom he had evidently led to Christ, so that he could call him 'my son whom I love, who is faithful in the Lord' (1 Cor. 4:17). It is also that he had grown to trust Timothy as his 'co-worker' (Rom. 16:21) and his 'brother and co-worker in God's service in spreading the gospel of Christ' (1 Thess. 3:2). Indeed, because of Timothy's genuine concern for the welfare of the churches and because of the loyalty with which 'as a son with his father' he had served with Paul in the gospel, Paul could go so far as to say 'I have no one else like him' (Phil. 2:20–22). Among all Paul's associates Timothy was unique.

It is not surprising, therefore, that when the first imprisonment was over Paul left Timothy in Ephesus as the accepted leader of the church, a kind of embryonic 'bishop'. Wide responsibilities were given him: to combat the heretics who were troubling the church there, to order the church's worship, to select and ordain its elders, to regularize the relief and ministry of its widows, to command and teach the apostolic faith, together with the moral duties which flow from it.[10] And now still heavier burdens were about to fall on Timothy's shoulders. For Paul was on the point of martyrdom, and then the task of preserving the apostle's teaching intact would be his in yet greater measure. Yet, humanly speaking, Timothy was hopelessly unfit to assume these weighty responsibilities of leadership in the church.

For one thing, Timothy was still comparatively young. Paul had urged him in his first letter: 'don't let anyone look down on you because you are young' (1 Tim. 4:12). And in his second letter a year or two later he warned him to 'flee the evil desires of youth' (2 Tim. 2:22). We do not know his precise age. If he had been about twenty years old when Paul enrolled him as a missionary associate, he would be in his mid thirties now. This period of life was regarded as belonging to youth,

> for there were only two recognized standards of age to the Greek
> or Roman, *neos* and *gerōn*, *juvenis* and *senex*, and the former of these
> conveyed no such juvenile implication as our term *youngster* . . . It was
> employed of adults in the full vigour of life and of soldiers of military
> age to the verge of forty.[11]

Certainly the thirties would be a young age for such church leadership as had been committed to Timothy.

Next, Timothy was prone to illness. In his first letter to him the apostle referred to his 'frequent illnesses', though without specifying what they were. He went on to recommend a tonic. For his stomach's sake, he advised, he should give up drinking only water and try a little wine as well (1 Tim. 5:23).

Third, Timothy was timid by temperament. He seems to have been naturally shy. If he had lived in our generation, I think we would have described him as an 'introvert'. He evidently shrank from difficult tasks, so that Paul in writing to the Corinthians had to pave the way for his mission: 'When Timothy comes, see to it that he has nothing to fear while he is with you.' Again, 'no one . . . should treat him with contempt' (1 Cor. 16:10–11). Several times in this second letter which the apostle wrote him, he encouraged him to take his share of suffering and not to be afraid or

---

10 See the contents of Paul's first letter to Timothy, with its varied instructions to a church leader.

11 Simpson, p. 8.

ashamed, since God has not given us a spirit of cowardice (e.g. 2 Tim. 1:7–8; 2:1, 3; 3:12; 4:5). These admonitions were evidently necessary. Paul knew Timothy's weaknesses. He could not forget his tears when they had parted (2 Tim. 1:4). In Fairbairn's words, Timothy was 'disposed to lean rather than to lead'.[12]

This, then, was Timothy – young in years, frail in physique, retiring in disposition – who nevertheless was called to exacting responsibilities in the church of God. Greatness was being thrust upon him, and like Moses and Jeremiah and a host of others before and after him, Timothy was exceedingly reluctant to accept it. Is someone who is reading these pages in a similar situation? You are young and weak and shy, and yet God is calling you to leadership? This letter has a special message for all timid Timothys.

4. Paul's preoccupation in writing to Timothy was with the gospel, the deposit of truth which had been revealed and committed to him by God

The apostle's own career of gospel work was virtually over. For thirty years or so he had faithfully preached the good news, planted churches, defended the truth and consolidated the work. Truly, he had 'fought the good fight . . . finished the race . . . kept the faith' (2 Tim. 4:7). Now nothing awaited him but the victor's wreath at the winning post. A prisoner now, he would be a martyr soon.

But what would happen to the gospel when he was dead and gone? The emperor Nero, bent on suppressing all secret societies, and misunderstanding the nature of the Christian church, seemed determined to destroy it. Heretics appeared to be on the increase. There had recently been an almost total Asian apostasy from Paul's teaching (2 Tim. 1:15). Bishop Moule goes so far as to write that 'Christianity . . . trembled, *humanly speaking*, on the verge of annihilation'.[13] Who, then, would do battle for the truth when Paul had laid down his life? This was the question which dominated and vexed his mind as he lay in chains, and to which he addressed himself in this letter. Already in his first letter he had pleaded with Timothy to keep safe the deposit: 'Timothy, guard what has been

---

12 Fairbairn, p. 314.
13 Moule, p. 18.

entrusted to your care' (1 Tim. 6:20). But since then the situation had worsened. So the apostle's appeal became more urgent. He reminded Timothy that the precious gospel was now committed to *him*, and that it was now *his* turn to assume responsibility for it, to preach and teach it, to defend it against attack and against falsification, and to ensure its accurate transmission to the generations yet to come. In each chapter Paul returned to the same basic concern, or some aspect of it. Indeed, we may summarize the message of the letter in terms of a fourfold charge:

Chapter 1: The charge to guard the gospel.
Guard the good deposit that was entrusted to you – guard it with the help of the Holy Spirit who lives in us (1:14).

Chapter 2: The charge to suffer for the gospel.
Join with me in suffering, like a good soldier of Jesus Christ . . . Remember Jesus Christ . . . This is my gospel, for which I am suffering even to the point of being chained like a criminal (2:3, 8–9).

Chapter 3: The charge to continue in the gospel.
Evildoers and impostors will go from bad to worse, deceiving and being deceived. But as for you, continue in what you have learned and have become convinced of (3:13–14).

Chapter 4: The charge to preach the gospel.
In the presence of God and of Christ Jesus . . . I give you this charge: preach the word; be prepared in season and out of season; correct, rebuke and encourage – with great patience and careful instruction (4:1–2).

The church of our day urgently needs to take to heart the message of this second letter of Paul to Timothy. For all around us we see Christians and churches relaxing their grasp of the gospel, fumbling it, in danger of letting it drop from their hands altogether. A new generation of young Timothys is needed, who will guard the sacred deposit of the gospel, who are determined to proclaim it and are prepared to suffer for it, and who will pass it on pure and uncorrupted to the generation which in due course will rise up to follow them.

2 Timothy 1:1–18

1. The charge to guard the gospel

Before the apostle reaches the main theme of this chapter, the charge to Timothy not to be ashamed of the gospel but rather to guard it safely (8–14), he begins his letter with the customary personal greeting (1–2), followed by a thanksgiving (3–5) and an exhortation (6–8). In this opening paragraph we are introduced in a very vivid way to both Paul and Timothy, the writer and the recipient of the letter. In particular, we are told something of how each of them had come to be what he was. These verses throw light on the providence of God, on how God fashions people into what he wants them to be.

1. Paul, an apostle of Christ Jesus (1:1)

In describing himself as *an apostle of Christ Jesus* Paul is making a considerable claim for himself. He is in fact ranking himself with the Twelve whom Jesus personally selected out of the wider company of his disciples. To them he gave the special title 'apostles' (Luke 6:13), indicating that he intended to send them out on their mission to represent him and to teach in his name. In order to equip them for this role, he arranged for them to be 'with him' (Mark 3:14). They would thus have unrivalled opportunities to hear his words and see his works, and so be in a position to bear witness to him and to everything they had seen and heard of him (John 15:27). He also promised them an extraordinary inspiration of the Holy Spirit to remind them of what he had taught them and to lead them into all the truth which he had not been able to teach them (John 14:25–26; 16:12–13).

Paul claims that he was later added to this select group. He saw the risen Lord on the Damascus road, which gave him the qualification every apostle needed: to be a witness to the resurrection (Acts 1:21–26; 1 Cor. 9:1; 15:8–9). Indeed, his Damascus road experience was more than his conversion; it was his commissioning as an apostle. Christ said to him:

> I have appeared to you to appoint you as a servant and as a witness of what you have seen and will see of me. I will rescue you from your own people and from the Gentiles. I am sending you to them to open their eyes.
> (Acts 26:16–18)

For the Lord's words 'I am sending you' were *ego apostellō se*, 'I apostle you', that is, 'I appoint you the apostle to the Gentiles' (cf. Rom. 11:13; Gal. 1:15–16; 2:9).

Paul could never forget this commissioning. He defended his apostolic mission and message against all his critics, insisting that his apostleship came from Christ and not from human beings (e.g. Gal. 1:1, 11–12). Even now, at the moment of writing, humiliated by people and awaiting the emperor's pleasure, this common prisoner is a privileged apostle of Christ Jesus, the King of kings.

Paul goes on to describe his apostleship in two ways, reminding Timothy of both its origin and its object.

Its origin was *the will of God*. He has used identical words (*dia thelēmatos theou*) at the beginning of both his letters to Corinth and the two prison letters to the Ephesians and Colossians. Indeed, in nine out of thirteen of his letters, including his first (to the Galatians) and his last (this one to Timothy), he refers either to the 'will' or the 'call' or the 'command' of God by which he has been made an apostle. It was his sustained conviction, from the beginning to the end of his apostolic career, that his appointment as an apostle had come neither from the church, nor from any human individual or group of people. Nor was he self-appointed. On the contrary, his apostleship originated in the eternal will and historical call of almighty God through Jesus Christ.

The object of his apostleship concerns *the promise of life that is in Christ Jesus*. That is to say, he had been commissioned as an apostle first to formulate and then to communicate the gospel. And the gospel is good news for dying sinners that God has promised them life in Jesus Christ. It seems particularly appropriate that, as death stares the apostle in the face, he should here define it as a *promise of life*. For this is what it is. The gospel offers people life – true life, eternal life – both here and hereafter. It declares that this life is *in Christ Jesus*, who not only said he was himself the life (John 14:6) but, as Paul will soon explain, actually 'destroyed death and brought life and immortality to light through the gospel' (10).

The gospel does more than 'offer' life; it 'promises' life to all who are in Christ. It says uncompromisingly: 'whoever has the Son has life' (1 John 5:12). Indeed, the whole Bible may fairly be described as a divine promise of life, from the first mention of 'the tree of life' in Genesis 3 to the last chapter of Revelation in which God's redeemed people eat of the tree of life and drink of the water of life freely. Eternal life is a gift 'which God, who does not lie, promised before the beginning of time', but has now made known through the preaching of the gospel (cf. verses 9–10; Titus 1:2–3; Rom. 1:1–2).

This, then, is how Paul introduces himself. He is an apostle of Christ Jesus. His apostleship originated in the will of God and has issued in the proclamation of the gospel of God, namely *the promise of life that is in Christ Jesus*.

2. Timothy, Paul's dear son (1:2–8)

Paul calls Timothy here *my dear son* and elsewhere 'my son whom I love' (1 Cor. 4:17) presumably because he has been the human instrument of Timothy's conversion. Certainly the reason he could describe the Corinthians as 'my dear children' was 'for in Christ Jesus I became your father through the gospel' (1 Cor. 4:14–15). We assume, therefore, that when Paul visited Lystra on the first missionary journey, 'where they continued to preach the gospel' (Acts 14:6–7), Timothy both heard and embraced the good news, so that, when Paul revisited Lystra a few years later on his second missionary journey, 'where a disciple named Timothy lived', Timothy had already made such progress in the Christian life that 'the believers at Lystra and Iconium spoke well of him' (Acts 16:1–2).

To his 'dear son' Paul now sends his usual greeting of *grace . . . and peace*, though adding in both letters to Timothy *mercy* as well. We may be sure that this threefold greeting is no mere stylistic convention, for these are significant theological words. They tell us much about both humanity's sorry condition in sin and God's great love for us all the same. For if *grace* is God's kindness to the undeserving, *mercy* is shown to the weak and helpless who cannot help themselves. In the parables of Jesus it was mercy which the good Samaritan showed to the robbers' victim and which the king extended to his servant who was so deeply in debt that he could not pay (Luke 10:37; Matt. 18:33). And it was mercy which had converted Saul of Tarsus, the old blasphemer and persecutor. 'I was shown mercy,' he had written in his earlier letter to Timothy (1 Tim. 1:13, 16). *Peace*, on the other hand, is reconciliation, the restoration of harmony to lives spoiled by discord. We may perhaps summarize these three blessings of God's love as being grace to the worthless, mercy to the helpless and peace to the restless, while *God the Father and Christ Jesus our Lord* together constitute the one spring from which this threefold stream flows.

There follows a very personal paragraph, in which the apostle assures Timothy that he constantly remembers him. *I constantly remember you in my prayers*, he says (3). *Recalling your tears . . .* (4). *I am reminded of your sincere faith* (5). And whenever I remember you, Timothy, *I thank God* (3).

This last point is significant. It indicates Paul's recognition that it was God who had made Timothy what he was. Timothy was not an apostle like Paul. They used to make this plain when they wrote letters to the churches together; for example, to the Colossians: 'Paul, an apostle of Christ Jesus by the will of God, and Timothy our brother'. Timothy was a Christian brother. He was also a Christian minister, a missionary and an apostolic delegate. And God had been at work in his life to make him all these things. Directly or indirectly in this paragraph Paul mentions the four major influences which have contributed to the shaping and making of Timothy.

a. His parental upbringing

Paul refers in this paragraph both to his own and to Timothy's *ancestors* (3) and to Timothy's mother and grandmother (5). This was right, for everyone is to a great extent the product of his or her inheritance. The most formative influence on each of us has been our parentage and our home. Hence good biographies never begin with their subjects, but with their parents, and probably their grandparents as well. True, we cannot inherit our parents' faith in the way that we inherit facets of their personalities. But a son or daughter can be led to faith through his or her parents' teaching, example and prayers.

Now Timothy had had a godly home. Luke tells us that he was the son of a mixed marriage, in that his father was Greek and his mother Jewish (Acts 16:1). Presumably his father was an unbeliever, but his mother Eunice was a believing Jewess who became a Christian. And before her his grandmother Lois had evidently been converted, for Paul can write of the *sincere faith* of all three generations (5). Perhaps grandmother, mother and son all owed their conversion to Paul when he brought the gospel to Lystra. Even before their conversion to Christ, however, these godly Jewish women had instructed Timothy out of the Old Testament, so that 'from infancy' he had 'known the Holy Scriptures' (3:15). Calvin's rather delightful comment is that Timothy 'was reared in his infancy in such a way that he could suck in godliness along with his mother's milk'.[1]

Paul could say much the same of himself. He was serving God *with a clear conscience*, as his forebears had done before him (3). Of course, his faith became richer, fuller and deeper when God had revealed Christ to him. Yet it was still substantially the same faith as that of Old Testament believers like Abraham and David, as he had argued in Romans 4, for it was the same God in whom they had all believed. No wonder he had been able to affirm to Felix the procurator: 'I worship the God of our ancestors' (Acts 24:14; cf. 26:6). We need to remember this when we are witnessing to Jewish people today. The conversion of Jews to Christ is not in any sense an act of disloyalty to their ancestors; it is rather the fulfilment of their ancestors' faith and hope.

Returning to Timothy, the first influence on him was his parental upbringing, and in particular a mother and a grandmother who were sincere believers and who had taught him out of the Scriptures from his childhood. Today also anyone who has been born and bred in a Christian home has received from God a blessing beyond price.

b. His spiritual friendship

After our parents it is our friends who influence us most, especially if they are also in some sense our teachers. And Timothy had in Paul an outstanding teacher-friend.

We have already seen that Paul was Timothy's spiritual 'father'. Having led him to Christ, however, he did not abandon or even forget him. No. He constantly 'remembered' him, as he says repeatedly in this passage.

---

[1] Calvin, p. 292. Cf. p. 242 for a similar comment on 1 Tim. 4:6.

He had also taken him with him on his journeys and trained him as his apprentice. When they had parted on the last occasion, Timothy had been unable to hold back his tears. And now, recalling his tears, Paul 'longed' to see him again, that he might again be *filled with joy* (4); he longed (as Bishop Handley Moule renders *epipothōn*) with 'homesick yearning'.[2] Meanwhile, he was praying for him *constantly* (3), and from time to time wrote him letters of advice and encouragement, like this one.

Such a Christian friendship, including the companionship, the letters and the prayers through which it was expressed, did not fail to have a powerful moulding effect on young Timothy, strengthening and sustaining him in his Christian life and service.

I thank God for the man who led me to Christ and for the extraordinary devotion with which he nurtured me in the early years of my Christian life. He wrote to me every week for, I think, seven years. He also prayed for me every day. I can only begin to guess what I owe, under God, to such a faithful friend and pastor.

c. His special endowment

Paul turns now from the indirect means God used to shape Timothy's Christian character (his parents and friends) to a direct gift which God has given him. *For this reason I remind you to fan into flame the gift of God, which is in you through the laying on of my hands* (6). What this gift of God's grace was, this *charisma*, we do not know with any certainty, for the very good reason that we are not told. We are not to go beyond Scripture. Nevertheless, we can hazard a guess, so long as we recognize its tentative nature. What is clear, both from this verse and from a similar reference in 1 Timothy 4:14, is that the gift was bestowed upon him when Paul and certain 'elders' (probably of the Lystra church) laid their hands on him. Both verses mention the laying-on of hands and seem to refer to what we might call his 'ordination' or 'commissioning'. If we are right so far, then the gift in question was an 'ordination gift', a gift related to his ministry. Paul may indeed be referring to the ministry itself, to which by the laying-on of hands Timothy was set apart. Certainly the offices of pastor and teacher, like those of apostle and prophet, are described as gifts of God's grace (Eph. 4:7, 11). So Dean Alford may be right to say that 'the spiritual gift is that of teaching and ruling the

---

2 Moule, pp. 40 and 45.

church'.[3] Or the reference may be to the gift of an evangelist, which work Paul will soon urge Timothy to do and so fulfil his ministry (4:5). Or again, since the apostle proceeds at once to refer to the kind of spirit God has given us (7), he may be referring to a special endowment or anointing of the Spirit which Timothy received at his ordination to equip him for the work to which he had been called. Speaking for myself, I think it is safest to describe Timothy's *charisma* in Alfred Plummer's words as 'the authority and power to be a minister of Christ'.[4] That is, it included both the office and the spiritual equipment needed to fulfil it.

We learn, then, that we are not only what we owe to our parents, friends and teachers, but what God himself has made us by calling us to some particular ministry and by endowing us with appropriate spiritual resources.

d. His personal discipline

Indeed, all God's gifts – natural and spiritual – need to be developed and used. Our Lord's parables of the bags of gold and the ten minas illustrate clearly the duty of service, the reward of faithfulness and the danger of laziness. So Paul tells Timothy in his first letter not to 'neglect' his gift (4:14) and in his second letter rather to *fan* it *into flame* (6). The gift is likened to a fire. The Greek verb *anazōpyreō*, which occurs nowhere else in the New Testament, does not necessarily imply that Timothy has let the fire die down and must now fan the dying embers into flame again. The prefix *ana* can indicate as much a stirring *up* as a *re*kindling. It seems, then, that Paul's appeal is to continue fanning it, to 'stir up that inner fire' (JBP), to keep it alive, even ablaze, presumably by exercising the gift faithfully and by waiting upon God in prayer for its constant renewal.

Having issued this appeal, Paul immediately adds his reason: *For the Spirit God gave us does not make us timid, but gives us power, love and self-discipline* (7). We have already considered the problems of youth, ill health and temperament with which timid Timothy had to battle. He appears to have been a very shy and sensitive individual, to whom responsibility was a heavy burden. Perhaps he was also fearful of spiritual excesses and extravagances. So Paul needs not only to urge him to keep stirring up his gift, but to reassure him that he need not be hesitant about exercising it.

---

[3] Alford, p. 342, a comment on 1 Tim. 4:14.

[4] Plummer, p. 314.

Why not? Well, because 'cowardliness has nothing to do with Christianity'.[5] Or, as Paul expresses it, because of the Spirit God has given us. Notice that, though a particular spiritual gift was given to *you*, Timothy, the gift of the Spirit himself has been given to *us*, to all of us who are in Christ. And this Spirit God has given to us all is a Spirit not of 'timidity' but of *power, love and self-discipline*. Since he is the Spirit of power we may be confident of his enabling as we exercise our ministry. Since he is the Spirit of love we must use God's authority and power in serving others, not in self-assertion or vainglory. And since he is the Spirit of self-discipline we must use them with appropriate reverence and restraint.

So far we have studied what the first seven verses of the letter tell us about these two men, Paul and Timothy, and their making. Paul claims to be Jesus Christ's apostle 'by the will of God', as previously he had said it was 'by the grace of God' that he was what he was (1 Cor. 15:10). And a whole complex of factors had made Timothy what he was – a godly upbringing, Paul's friendship and training, God's gift to him, and his own self-discipline in stirring it up.

In principle, it is the same with all God's people. Perhaps the most striking thing is the combination of divine sovereignty and human responsibility in both Paul and Timothy, those two facts of revelation and experience which we find it difficult to reconcile and impossible to systematize into a tidy doctrine.

Paul could write of God's will and assert that God's grace had made him what he was. But then he would at once add: 'and his grace to me was not without effect. No, I worked harder than all of them – yet not I, but the grace of God that was with me' (1 Cor. 15:10). That is, he added his labour to God's grace, although, to be sure, it was God's grace which inspired his labour.

Timothy was similar. His mother and grandmother could teach him out of the Scriptures and lead him towards conversion. Paul could actually bring him to Christ, befriend him, pray for him, write to him, train and exhort him. And God could give him a special gift at his ordination. But still Timothy must himself stir up the divine gift within him. He must add his own self-discipline to God's gifts.

---

5 Barrett, p. 94.

We are no different. However much (or little) we may have received from God, either directly in natural and spiritual endowment or indirectly through parents, friends and teachers, we must still apply ourselves in active self-discipline to cooperate with God's grace, to keep fanning the inner fire into flame. Otherwise, we shall never be the men and women God wants us to be, or fulfil the ministry he has given us to exercise.

Paul now turns from the varied factors which have contributed to the making of Timothy to the truth of the gospel and to Timothy's responsibility in relation to the gospel. Before he defines the gospel, he begs Timothy not to be ashamed of it (8). Suffering rather than shame is to characterize Timothy's ministry. He may be young, frail, timid and weak. He may shrink from the tasks to which he is being called. But God has moulded and gifted him for his ministry. So he must not be ashamed or afraid to exercise it.

This means, to begin with, that Timothy must *not be ashamed* of Christ, *of the testimony about our Lord*. Every Christian is Christ's witness, and Christian testimony is essentially testimony to or about Christ (cf. John 15:26–27; Acts 1:8). So every Christian must be ready and willing, if necessary, to be a 'fool for Christ' (1 Cor. 4:10); we need not be prepared to be a fool for anyone else!

If Timothy must not be ashamed of the Lord, he must not be ashamed of Paul either. For it is possible to be proud of Christ, but ashamed of his people and embarrassed to be associated with them. It seems that when Paul was re-arrested and put in chains, nearly all his former supporters forsook him (15). He now begs Timothy not to follow suit. He may be the emperor's prisoner in the eyes of others; he is the Lord's prisoner in reality, his willing captive, and held in prison by human beings only by Christ's permission and for Christ's sake.[6]

Timothy must also not be ashamed of the gospel, but rather take his share of suffering for it. Weak as he was in himself, he could be strengthened by the power of God to endure it. For endure suffering he must, since the gospel of Christ crucified, foolishness to some and a stumbling block to others (1 Cor. 1:23), always arouses opposition. And

---

[6] During his earlier house arrest in Rome Paul called himself a (or the) 'prisoner of Christ Jesus' in Eph. 3:1 and Phlm. 1, 9, just as here he is *his prisoner*, while in Eph. 4:1 the expression he used was 'the prisoner in the Lord' (*en kyriō*), meaning perhaps that he had been imprisoned because of his union with Christ.

opposing the message, people naturally oppose its messengers, who thus 'suffer with the suffering gospel'.[7]

These are still the three main ways in which Christian people, like Timothy, are tempted to feel ashamed: now of the *name* of Christ, to whom we are called to witness, now of the *people* of Christ, to whom we also belong if we belong to him, and now of the *gospel* of Christ, which is entrusted to us to spread.

The temptation is strong and subtle. If Timothy had not felt it, Paul would not have encouraged him in these terms. If Paul himself had never felt it, it would have been unnecessary for him some years previously to assert so strongly, 'For I am not ashamed of the gospel, because it is the power of God that brings salvation to everyone who believes' (Rom. 1:16). Indeed, if this were not a temptation common to all of us, the Lord Jesus would not have needed to issue the solemn warning, 'If anyone is ashamed of me and my words in this adulterous and sinful generation, the Son of Man will be ashamed of them when he comes in his Father's glory with the holy angels' (Mark 8:38). We are all more sensitive to public opinion than we like to admit, and tend to bow down too readily before its pressure, like reeds shaken by the wind.

Paul now enlarges on the gospel of which Timothy is not to be ashamed, and for which he must take his share of suffering. He begins by sketching its main features (9–10) and then summarizes our responsibility in relation to it (11–18). This, then, is the double theme of the rest of the chapter: God's gospel and our duty.

3. God's gospel (1:9–10)

It is striking to hear Paul pass at once from a reference to 'the gospel' to the central affirmation *God . . . saved us*. For it is really impossible to speak of the gospel without going on in the same breath to speak of salvation. The gospel is precisely this, good news of salvation, or good news *of our Saviour, Christ Jesus* (10). Ever since the good news of great joy was first announced on Christmas Day in terms of the birth of 'a Saviour . . . [who] is the Messiah, the Lord' (Luke 2:10–11), the followers of Jesus have

---

[7] Moule, pp. 45, 72.

recognized its essential content. Paul himself never wavered. In Pisidian Antioch during the first missionary journey he referred to his gospel as 'this message of salvation'. In Philippi during the second missionary journey he and his companions were described as 'servants of the Most High God, who are telling you the way to be saved'. And writing to the Ephesians from Rome he called the word of truth 'the gospel of your salvation' (Acts 13:26; 16:17; Eph. 1:13).

So here, as Paul writes about the gospel, the terminology which he has made familiar recurs, namely that we are saved in Christ Jesus by God's purpose, grace and call, and not by our own works. For he is explaining the same gospel in his last letter (2 Timothy) as he set out in his first (Galatians). His gospel has not changed with the passing years. There is only one gospel of salvation. And although both words 'gospel' and 'salvation' need today to be translated into terms meaningful to modern people, we have no freedom to alter the substance of our message. As we come to look more closely at the concise statement of God's gospel which he makes in these verses, we shall see that he indicates its character (what it is), its source (where it comes from) and its ground (on what it rests).

a. The character of salvation

We need to bring together the three clauses which assert that he *saved us*, he *called us to a holy life* and he *brought life and immortality to light*. For these make it plain that salvation is far more than forgiveness. The God who *saved* us also and simultaneously *called us to a holy life*. The Christian calling is a holy calling. When God calls us to himself, he calls us to holiness also. Paul has laid much emphasis on this in his earlier letters. 'God did not call us to be impure, but to live a holy life.' For all of us are 'called to be his holy people', called to live as the holy, the separated, people of God (1 Thess. 4:7; 1 Cor. 1:2). But if holiness is an integral part of God's plan of salvation, so is the *immortality* of which he writes in the following verse (10). Indeed, 'forgiveness', 'holiness' and 'immortality' are all three aspects of God's great 'salvation'.

The term 'salvation' urgently needs to be rescued from the mean and meagre concepts to which we tend to degrade it. 'Salvation' is a majestic word, denoting that comprehensive purpose of God by which he justifies, sanctifies and glorifies his people: first pardoning our offences and accepting us as righteous in his sight through Christ, then progressively transforming us by his Spirit into the image of his Son, until finally we

21

become like Christ in heaven, with new bodies in a new world. We must not minimize the greatness of 'so great a salvation' (Heb. 2:3).

b. The source of salvation

Where does such a great salvation come from? Paul answers, *not because of anything we have done but because of his own purpose and grace. This grace was given us in Christ Jesus before the beginning of time* (9). If we want to trace the river of salvation to its source, we must look right back beyond time to a past eternity. The apostle's actual words are 'before eternal times'.[8]

In order to put beyond question the truth that God's predestination and election belong to eternity and not to time, Paul uses an aorist participle to indicate that God actually gave us something (*dotheisan*) from all eternity in Christ. What he gave us was *his own purpose and grace*, for a way of expressing 'his own purpose of grace'. His saving purpose was not arbitrary, but gracious.[9] It is plain, therefore, that the source of our salvation is not our own works. For God gave us his own purpose of grace in Christ before we did any good works, before we were born and could do any good works, indeed before history, before time, in eternity.

We have to agree that the doctrine of election is difficult to finite minds. But it is undoubtedly a biblical doctrine. It emphasizes that salvation is due to God's grace alone, not to human merit; not to our works performed in time, but to God's purpose conceived in eternity. Thus understood, God's purpose of election is bound to be mysterious to us, for we cannot hope to understand the secret thoughts and decisions of the mind of God. However, the doctrine of election is never introduced in Scripture either to arouse or to baffle our natural curiosity, but always for a practical purpose. On the one hand, it generates deep humility and gratitude, for it excludes all boasting. On the other, it brings both peace and assurance, for nothing can quieten our fears for our own stability like the knowledge that our safety depends ultimately not on ourselves but on God's own purpose of grace.

c. The ground of salvation

Our salvation rests firmly grounded upon the historical work performed by Jesus Christ at his first appearing. For though God 'gave' us his grace in

---

[8] *Pro chronōn aiōniōn*. The same expression occurs in Titus 1:2 with reference to God's promise of life. Cf. Rom. 16:25.

[9] See Rom. 8:28; 9:11; and Eph. 1:11 for other examples of God's predestinating, saving 'purpose' (*prothesis*).

Christ Jesus *before the beginning of time*, he *revealed* it in time, *now*, through the appearing of the same Christ Jesus, our Saviour. Both divine stages were in and through Jesus Christ, but the giving was eternal and secret, while the revealing was historical and public.

What, then, did Christ do when he appeared and proceeded to reveal God's eternal purpose of grace? To this Paul gives a double answer in verse 10. First, Jesus Christ *destroyed death*. Second, he *brought life and immortality to light through the gospel*.

First, Christ *destroyed death*. *Death* is, in fact, the one word which summarizes our human predicament as a result of sin. For death is the 'wage' sin pays, its grim penalty (Rom. 6:23). And this is true of each form which death takes. For Scripture speaks of death in three ways. There is physical death, the separation of the soul from the body. There is spiritual death, the separation of the soul from God. And there is eternal death, the separation of both soul and body from God for ever. All are due to sin; they are sin's terrible though just reward.

But Jesus Christ *destroyed* death. This cannot mean that he eliminated it, as we know from our everyday experience. Sinners are still 'dead in [their] transgressions and sins' in which they live (Eph. 2:1–2) until God makes them alive in Christ. All human beings die physically and will continue to do so, with the exception of the generation who are alive when Christ returns in glory. And some are going to die 'the second death', which is one of the fearful expressions used in the book of Revelation for hell (e.g. Rev. 20:14; 21:8). Indeed, Paul has written previously that the final eradication of death still lies in the future, as the last enemy of God to be destroyed (1 Cor. 15:26). Not until the return of Christ and the resurrection of the dead shall we be able to shout with joy, 'Death has been swallowed up in victory' (1 Cor. 15:54; cf. Rev. 21:4).

What is triumphantly asserted in this verse by Paul is that at his first appearing Christ decisively 'defeated' or 'overthrew' death. The Greek verb *katargeō* is not in itself conclusive, for it can be used with a variety of meanings, which must be determined by the context. Nevertheless, its first and foremost meaning is 'make ineffective, powerless, idle' or 'nullify' (AG). So Paul can liken death to a scorpion whose sting has been drawn and to a military commander whose army has been defeated, and can cry out with defiance: 'Where, O death, is your victory? Where, O death, is your sting?' (1 Cor. 15:55). For Christ 'has broken the power of death' (AG, NEB).

It is surely significant that this same verb *katargeō* is used in the New Testament with reference to the devil and to our fallen nature as well as to death (Heb. 2:14; Rom. 6:6). Neither the devil, nor our fallen nature, nor death has been annihilated. But by the power of Christ the tyranny of each has been broken, so that if we are in Christ we can be set free.

Consider in particular how Christ has *destroyed* or 'nullified' death.

Physical death is no longer the grim ogre it once seemed to us and still seems to many whom Christ has not yet liberated. Their 'fear of death' holds them 'in slavery' (Heb. 2:15). But for Christian believers death is simply 'falling asleep' in Christ. It is, in fact, a positive 'gain', because it is the gateway to being 'with Christ' which is 'better by far'. It is one of the possessions which become 'ours' when we are Christ's (1 Thess. 4:14–15; Phil. 1:21, 23; 1 Cor. 3:22–23). It has been rendered so innocuous that Jesus could even state that believers, though they die, 'will never die' (John 11:25–26). What is absolutely certain is that death will never be able to separate us from God's love in Christ (Rom. 8:38–39).

Spiritual death has, for Christian believers, given way to that eternal life which is communion with God begun on earth and perfected in heaven. Further, those who are in Christ will 'not be hurt at all by the second death', for they have already 'crossed over from death to life' (Rev. 2:11; John 5:24; 1 John 3:14).

Second, *Christ brought life and immortality to light through the gospel.* This is the positive counterpart. It is by his death and resurrection that Christ destroyed death. It is through the gospel that he now reveals what he has done, and offers us the life and immortality which he has won for us. Whether we should distinguish between the words *life* and *immortality* is not clear. They may mean the same, the second word defining the first. That is, the kind of life Christ has secured for us, and now discloses and offers through the gospel, is eternal life, a life that is immortal and incorruptible. Only God possesses immortality in himself. But Christ gives it to human beings. Even our bodies after the resurrection will share in this immortality (1 Cor. 15:42, 52–54). So will the inheritance which we shall receive (1 Pet. 1:4). On the other hand, as C. K. Barrett writes: 'possibly "life" refers to the new life made available in this world, "immortality" to its prolongation after death'.[10] Whichever way we take the words, both are 'revealed' or *brought . . . to light* through the gospel. There are many hints

---

[10] Barrett, p. 95.

in Old Testament Scripture about a life after death, and a few bright flashes of faith, but on the whole the Old Testament revelation was what Bishop Moule called a 'comparative dusk'.[11] Now, however, the gospel has thrown floods of light upon the offer of immortal life through Christ's conquest of death.

In order to appreciate the full force of this Christian affirmation, we need to call to mind who it is who is making it. Who is this who writes so confidently about life and death, about the destruction of death and the revelation of life? It is one who is facing the prospect of imminent death himself. Any day now he expects to receive the death sentence. Already the final summons is ringing in his ears. Already he can see in his imagination the flash of the executioner's sword. And yet, in the very presence of death, he can shout aloud: 'Christ has destroyed death.' This is Christian faith triumphant!

How we long for the contemporary church to recover its lost certainty about the victory of Jesus Christ and to declare this good news to a world for whom death is the great unmentionable. *The Observer* magazine devoted a whole issue to death in October 1968 and commented:

> Far from being prepared for death, modern society has made the very word almost unmentionable . . . we have brought all our talents into use to avoid the prospect of dying – and when the time comes we may react with anything from excessive triviality to total despair.

One of the most searching tests to apply to any religion concerns its attitude to death. And measured by this test much so-called Christianity is found wanting with its black clothes, its mournful chants and its requiem masses. Of course dying can be very unpleasant, and bereavement can bring bitter sorrow. But death itself has been overthrown, and 'blessed are the dead who die in the Lord' (Rev. 14:13). The proper epitaph to write for a Christian believer is not a dismal and uncertain petition, 'R.I.P.' (*requiescat in pace*, 'may he or she rest in peace'), but a joyful and certain affirmation 'C.A.D.' ('Christ abolished death')!

Such, then, is the salvation which is offered us in the gospel and which is ours in Christ. Its *character* is our recreation and transformation into the

---

[11] Moule, p. 50.

holiness of Christ here and hereafter. Its *source* is God's eternal purpose of grace. Its *ground* is Christ's historical appearing and abolition of death.

Putting these great truths together, we can detect five stages by which God's saving purpose unfolds. The first is the eternal gift to us in Christ of his grace. The second is the historical appearing of Christ to destroy death by his death and resurrection. The third is the personal call of God to sinners through the preaching of the gospel. The fourth is the moral sanctification of believers by the Holy Spirit. And the fifth is the final heavenly perfection in which the holy calling is completed.

The sweep of God's purpose of grace is majestic indeed, as Paul traces it from a past eternity through a historical outworking in Jesus Christ and in the Christian to an ultimate destiny with Christ and like Christ in a future immortality. Is it not truly wonderful that, although Paul's body is confined within the narrow limits of an underground cell, his heart and mind can thus soar into eternity?

4. Our duty in relation to God's gospel (1:11–18)

If we were to ask Paul what someone's first duty is in relation to the gospel, he would of course say to receive it and live by it. But his concern here is not with the duty of unbelievers, but with the duty of Christians towards the gospel after they have themselves embraced it. In answer to this question Paul gives three answers.

a. Our duty to communicate the gospel (1:11)

If the 'life and immortality' which Christ achieved are 'brought . . . to light through the gospel', then of course it is imperative that we should proclaim the gospel. So Paul continues: *And of this gospel I was appointed a herald and an apostle and a teacher.* The same combination of words occurs in 1 Timothy 2:7, and in both Paul uses the emphatic *egō*, no doubt to express his 'sense of personal wonder'[12] that he should have been given this privilege.

Perhaps we can relate the three offices of *apostle, herald* and *teacher* by saying that the apostles formulated the gospel, heralds proclaim it, and teachers instruct people systematically in its doctrines and in its ethical implications.

---

[12] Guthrie, p. 73.

There are no apostles of Christ today. We have already seen how restricted is the New Testament use of this term. The gospel was formulated by the apostles and has now been bequeathed by them to the church. It is found in its definitive form in the New Testament. This apostolic New Testament faith is authoritative for the church of every age and place. The church is 'built on the foundation of the apostles and prophets' (Eph. 2:20). There is no other gospel. There can be no new gospel.

Although there are no apostles of Christ today, there are certainly heralds and teachers, men and women called by God to devote themselves to the work of preaching and teaching. Notice that what they are called both to proclaim and to teach is the gospel. It is fashionable in theological circles to distinguish sharply between the *kērygma* (what was preached) and the *didachē* (what was taught), the *kērygma* being essentially the good news of Christ crucified and risen, with the summons to repent and believe, and the *didachē* being largely ethical instruction to converts. The distinction is useful, but can be made too much of. It is safe only if we remember how much they overlapped. There was a lot of *didachē* in the *kērygma* and a lot of *kērygma* in the *didachē*. And, moreover, both concerned the gospel, for the *kērygma* was the proclamation of its essence, while the *didachē* included the great doctrines which undergird it as well as the moral behaviour which follows from it.

The reference to 'testimony' in verse 8, which we have already considered, adds a fourth word to this list. It reminds us that, although there are no apostles today, and although only some are called to the ministry of preaching and teaching, all Christian believers are to be witnesses and to testify to Jesus Christ out of their own personal experience.

b. Our duty to suffer for the gospel (1:12a)

Paul has already summoned Timothy not to be ashamed but to take his share of suffering for the gospel (8), and he will enlarge on this theme in the second chapter of his letter. But now he emphasizes that he is not asking from Timothy something he is not prepared to experience himself: *That is why I am suffering as I am. Yet this is no cause for shame.* What is the reason for this link between suffering and the gospel? What is there about the gospel which people hate and oppose, and on account of which those who preach it have to suffer?

Just this: God saves sinners because of his own purpose and grace, and not because of their good works (9). It is the undeserved freeness of the gospel which offends. As 'natural' or unregenerate human beings we hate to have to admit the gravity of our sin and guilt, our complete helplessness to save ourselves, the indispensable necessity of God's grace and Christ's sin-bearing death to save us, and therefore our inescapable indebtedness to the cross. This is what Paul meant by 'the stumbling block of the cross'. Many preachers succumb to the temptation to downplay it. They preach human merit instead of Christ and his cross, and they substitute the one for the other 'to avoid being persecuted for the cross of Christ' (Gal. 6:12; cf. 5:11). No-one can preach Christ crucified with faithfulness and escape opposition, even persecution.

c. Our duty to guard the gospel (1:12b–18)

Leaving aside for the moment the second part of verse 12, we come to Paul's double appeal to Timothy in the next two verses: *What you heard from me, keep as the pattern of sound teaching* (13); *Guard the good deposit that was entrusted to you* (14). Here Paul refers to the gospel, the apostolic faith, by two expressions. It is both a pattern of sound teaching (13) and a precious deposit (14).

Sound teaching is 'healthy' teaching, the Greek expression being used in the Gospels of people whom Jesus healed. Previously they had been maimed or diseased; now they were well or 'whole'. So the Christian faith is 'the sound doctrine' (4:3), because it is not maimed or diseased but 'whole'. It is what Paul had previously called 'the whole will of God' (Acts 20:27).

Further, this *sound teaching* had been given by Paul to Timothy in a *pattern*. Here the Greek word is *hypotypōsis*. The NEB translates it 'outline', and Dr Guthrie says it 'means an outline sketch such as an architect might make before getting down to the detailed plans of a building'.[13] In this case Paul is implying that Timothy must amplify, expound and apply the apostle's teaching. The context, especially the parallel with the next verse, seems to me to make this an unlikely explanation. The only other occurrence of *hypotypōsis* in the New Testament is in Paul's first letter to Timothy where he describes himself, the object of Christ's amazing mercy and perfect patience, as 'an *example* for those who would believe in him' (1:16). Arndt and Gingrich, who give 'model' or 'example' as the usual translation, suggest that it is used 'rather in the sense *prototype*' in

---

[13] Guthrie, p. 132.

1 Timothy 1:16 and 'rather in the sense *standard*' in 2 Timothy 1:13. In this case Paul is commanding Timothy to keep before him as his standard of sound teaching what he has heard from the apostle. This certainly suits the general teaching of the letter and faithfully reflects the emphasis of the sentence on the first word 'model' or 'standard'.

So Paul's teaching is to be Timothy's guide or rule. He is not to depart from it. He is to follow it, or better, to hold it fast (*eche*). And he must do so *with faith and love in Christ Jesus*. That is, Paul is concerned not just with *what* Timothy is to do, but with *how* he does it. His personal doctrinal convictions and his instruction of others, as he grips hold of Paul's teaching, are to be characterized by faith and love. He is to seek these qualities from Christ – a sincere belief and a tender charity.

The apostolic faith is not only 'a standard of sound teaching'; it is also *the good deposit* (*hē kalē parathēkē*). For the gospel is a treasure – a good, noble and precious treasure – deposited for safe keeping with the church. Christ has entrusted it to Paul, and Paul now entrusts it to Timothy.

Timothy is to *guard* it. Paul has addressed precisely the same appeal to him at the end of his first letter (6:20), except that now he calls it the *good*, literally the 'beautiful', deposit. The verb (*phylassō*) means to guard something 'so that it is not lost or damaged' (AG). It is used of guarding a palace against marauders and possessions against thieves (Luke 11:21; Acts 22:20). There were heretics abroad, bent on corrupting the gospel and so robbing the church of the priceless treasure which had been entrusted to it. Timothy must be on the watch.

And he must guard the gospel all the more tenaciously because of what had happened in and around Ephesus (the capital of the Roman province of Asia) where Timothy was (15). The aorist tense of the verb *deserted me* seems to refer to some particular event. The most likely reference is to the moment of the apostle's re-arrest. The churches of Asia, where he had laboured for several years, had depended heavily upon him. Perhaps his arrest seemed to them to indicate that the Christian cause was now lost. Perhaps they reacted by rejecting and disowning him. We know nothing of *Phygelus* and *Hermogenes*, but their mention suggests they were the ringleaders. In any case Paul saw the turning away of the Asian churches as more than a personal desertion; it was a denial of his apostolic authority. It must have seemed particularly tragic because a few years previously, during Paul's two and a half years' residence in Ephesus, Luke says that 'all the Jews and Greeks who lived in the province of Asia heard the word of the Lord' and many believed (Acts 19:10). Now *everyone in . . . Asia* had turned away from him. The great awakening had been followed by a great defection. 'To every eye but that of faith it must have appeared just then as if the gospel were on the eve of extinction.'[14]

The one bright exception appears to have been a man called Onesiphorus, who had often entertained Paul in his home (*refreshed* him, 16), and had rendered him some other, unspecified service in Ephesus (18). He had thus been true to the meaning of his name, 'a bringer of profit'. In addition, he had not been ashamed of Paul's chains (16), which seems to mean both that he did not repudiate him at the time of his arrest, and that he then followed him, even accompanied him, to Rome, and then searched diligently for him until he found him in his dungeon. Paul had good reason to be grateful for this faithful and courageous friend. It is not surprising, therefore, that he twice utters a prayer (16, 18), first for his household (*may the Lord show mercy to the household of Onesiphorus*) and then for Onesiphorus himself (*may the Lord grant that he will find mercy from the Lord on that day*).

Various commentators, especially Roman Catholics, have argued from the references to the household of Onesiphorus (mentioned again in 4:19) and to *that day* that Onesiphorus himself was now dead, and that we have therefore in verse 18 a petition for the departed. This is an entirely unwarranted assumption, however. The fact that Paul keeps distinct his references to Onesiphorus on the one hand and to his household on the other could equally well mean that they were separated from each other by distance as by death, Onesiphorus being still in Rome, while his family were at home in Ephesus. 'I take it to be a prayer for them separately, the man and his family,' writes Bishop Handley Moule,

> because they were for the time separated from one another by lands and seas . . . There is no need at all to assume that Onesiphorus had died. Separation from his family by a journey quite satisfies the language of the passage.[15]

At all events, everybody in Asia, as Timothy was keenly aware, had turned away from the apostle, with the exception of loyal Onesiphorus

---

[14] Moule, p. 16.
[15] Moule, pp. 67, 68.

and his family. It was in such a situation of almost universal apostasy that Timothy was to *guard the good deposit*, to *keep . . . the pattern of sound teaching*, that is to say, to preserve the gospel unsullied and unalloyed. It would have been a heavy responsibility for anyone, let alone someone of Timothy's temperament. How, then, could he stand firm?

The apostle gives Timothy the reassurance he needs. He cannot hope to guard the gospel-treasure by himself; he can do it only *with the help of the Holy Spirit who lives in us* (14b). The same truth is taught in the second part of verse 12, which so far we have not considered. Many Christians are familiar with the AV rendering 'for I know whom I have believed, and am persuaded that he is able to keep that which I have committed unto him against that day'. These words are true, for many biblical passages confirm them, and, linguistically speaking, they are accurately translated. But the context makes another interpretation more probable. The AV words 'that which I have committed unto him' are a rendering of 'my deposit' (*tēn parathēkēn mou*). Indeed, both the verb ('guard') and the noun ('deposit') are precisely the same in verse 12 as in verse 14 and in 1 Timothy 6:20. The presumption is therefore that 'my deposit' is not what I have committed to him (my soul or myself, as in 1 Pet. 4:19) but what he has committed to me (the gospel).

The sense, then, is this. The deposit is 'mine', Paul could say, because Christ had committed it to him. Yet Paul was persuaded that Christ would himself keep it safe *until that day* when he would have to give an account of his stewardship. What was the ground of his confidence? Just this: 'I know him.' Paul knew Christ in whom he had put his trust and was convinced of his ability to keep the deposit safe: *I know whom I have believed, and am convinced that he is able to guard* what has been entrusted to me *until that day* (12). He has entrusted it to me, it is true; but he will take care of it himself. And now that Paul is entrusting it to Timothy, Timothy can be sustained by the same assurance.

There is great encouragement here. Ultimately, it is God himself who is the guarantor of the gospel. It is his responsibility to preserve it. 'On no other ground would the work of preaching be for a moment endurable.'[16] We may see the evangelical faith, the faith of the gospel, spoken against everywhere, and the apostolic message of the New Testament ridiculed. We may have to watch an increasing apostasy in the church, as our

---

[16] Barrett, p. 97.

generation abandons the faith of past generations. Do not be afraid! God will never allow the light of the gospel to be finally extinguished. True, he has committed it to us, frail and fallible creatures. He has placed his treasure in brittle, earthenware vessels. And we must play our part in guarding and defending the truth. Nevertheless, in entrusting the deposit to our hands, he has not taken his own hands off it. He is himself its final guardian, and *he* will preserve the truth which he has committed to the church. We know this because we know him in whom we have trusted and continue to trust.

We have seen that the gospel is good news of salvation, promised from eternity, secured by Christ in time, offered to faith.

Our first duty is to *communicate* this gospel, to use old ways and seek fresh ways of making it known throughout the whole world.

If we do so, we shall undoubtedly *suffer* for it, for the authentic gospel has never been popular. It humbles the sinner too much.

And when we are called to suffer for the gospel, we are tempted to trim it, to eliminate those elements which give offence and cause opposition, to mute the notes which jar on sensitive modern ears.

But we must resist the temptation. For, above all, we are called to *guard* the gospel, keeping it pure whatever the cost, and preserving it against every corruption.

Guard it faithfully. Spread it actively. Suffer for it bravely. This is our threefold duty to the gospel of God as expounded in this first chapter.

2 Timothy 2:1–26

2. The charge to suffer for the gospel

1. Handing on the truth (2:1–2)

The first chapter ended with Paul's sorrowful reference to the widespread defection among Christians in the Roman province of Asia (1:15). Onesiphorus and his household seem to have been the outstanding exceptions. Now Paul urges Timothy that he too, in the midst of the general landslide, must stand his ground. It is the first of several similar exhortations in the letter beginning *sy oun* or *sy de*, meaning 'you therefore' or 'but you', which summon Timothy to resist the prevailing mood. Timothy had been called to responsible leadership in the church not only in spite of his natural reticence but in the very area where the apostle's authority was being rejected. It is as if Paul says to him: 'Never mind what other people may be thinking or saying or doing. Never mind how weak and shy you yourself may feel. As for you, Timothy, be strong!'

Of course, if his encouragement had stopped there, it would have been futile, even absurd. He might as well have told a snail to be quick or a horse to fly as command a man as timid as Timothy to be strong. But Paul's call is Christian, not stoical. It is not a summons to Timothy to be strong in himself – to set his jaw and grit his teeth – but to 'be inwardly strengthened'[1] by means of *the grace that is in Christ Jesus*. The NEB expands the sentence like this: 'Take strength from the grace of God which is ours in Christ Jesus.' Timothy is to find his resources for ministry

---

[1] I take the verb as being 'simply passive' (Ellicott, p. 121), although it might be the middle voice, 'strengthen yourself inwardly'. The same verb occurs passively in Eph. 6:10 and actively in Phil. 4:13 and 2 Tim. 4:17.

not in his own nature but in Christ's grace. It is not only for salvation that we are dependent on grace (1:9), but for service also.

Paul goes on to indicate the kind of ministry for which Timothy will need to strengthen himself by Christ's grace. So far he has been urged to hold the faith and guard the deposit (1:13–14). He is to do more than preserve the truth, however; he is also to pass it on. If the disloyalty of the Asian church made it essential that Timothy should guard the truth with loyalty, the approaching death of the apostle made it equally important that Timothy should make arrangements for the handing down of the truth intact to the next generation. In this transmission of truth from hand to hand Paul sees four stages.

First, the faith has been entrusted to Paul by Christ. It is his by deposit, not by invention. As an apostle of Jesus Christ he insists that his gospel is not human in origin, whether his own composition or somebody else's. Nor is he relying purely on human tradition. On the contrary, he could write: 'I did not receive it from any man, nor was I taught it; rather, I received it by revelation from Jesus Christ' (Gal. 1:11–12).

Second, what has been entrusted to Paul by Christ Paul in his turn has entrusted to Timothy, 'the good deposit that was entrusted to you' (1:14). This deposit consists of certain 'sound teaching' which Timothy has heard from Paul's own lips. The exact expression 'what you heard from me' (1:13, *par' emou ēkousas*) is repeated in 2:2, though now with the addition that Timothy has heard it *in the presence of many witnesses.* The aorist tense would seem to refer not to a single public occasion on which Timothy heard the apostle's teaching – such as his baptism or ordination – but rather to the entirety of his instruction over the years. And the reference to the *many witnesses* shows that the apostolic faith was not a secret tradition handed on privately to Timothy (such as the Gnostics were claiming), whose authenticity there was no means of testing, but a public instruction, whose truth was guaranteed by the many witnesses who had heard it and who could therefore check Timothy's teaching against the apostle's.

This statement of Paul's became important in the following century when Gnosticism had grown and spread. For example, in chapter 25 of his *Prescriptions against Heretics* (c. AD 200) Tertullian of Carthage was writing particularly against Gnostics who claimed both to have had private revelations of their own and to possess secret traditions handed down from the apostles. He would not accept that the apostles had 'entrusted some things openly to all and some things secretly to a few'.

For (he argued) in appealing to Timothy to guard the deposit 'there is no hinting at a hidden doctrine, but a command not to admit any but the teaching which he had heard from Paul himself and (I think) openly – "before many witnesses" as he says'.[2]

Third, what Timothy has heard from Paul he is now to *entrust to reliable people*, of whom there are evidently some left among the many deserters of Asia. Those Paul has in mind must be primarily ministers of the word, whose chief function is to teach, Christian elders whose responsibility it would be – like the Jewish elders of the synagogue – to preserve the tradition. Such Christian elders are those who manage God's household, as Paul has recently written to Titus (1:7), because both God's household and God's truth are committed to their trust. And the fundamental requirement in such people is trustworthiness (1 Cor. 4:1–2). They must be *reliable people*.

Fourth, they must be the sort of people who (as the relative *hoitines* should be translated) *will also be qualified to teach others*. The ability or competence which Timothy must look for in such people will consist partly in their integrity or faithfulness of character already mentioned and partly in their ability to teach. They must be *didaktikoi*, 'apt teachers', a word Paul has used of candidates for the ministry in 1 Timothy 3:2 and will use again later in this chapter (2:24).

Here, then, are the four stages in the handing on of the truth which Paul has in mind: from Christ to Paul, from Paul to Timothy, from Timothy to *reliable people*, and from *reliable people* to *others*. This is the true 'apostolic succession'. Certainly it would involve a line of 'reliable people', but the succession from the apostles is to be more in the message itself than in the people who teach it. It is to be a succession of apostolic tradition rather than of apostolic ministry, authority or order, a transmission of the apostles' doctrine handed down unchanged from the apostles to subsequent generations, and passed from hand to hand like the Olympic torch. This apostolic tradition, 'the good deposit', is now to be found in the New Testament. Speaking ideally, 'Scripture' and 'tradition' should be interchangeable terms, for what the church hands down from generation to generation should be the biblical faith, no more and no less. And the biblical faith is the apostolic faith.

---

[2] *Early Latin Theology*, edited by S. L. Greenslade (vol. 5 of the SCM Library of Christian Classics, 1956), p. 47.

In the rest of this second chapter of his letter Paul enlarges on the teaching ministry to which Timothy has been called. He illustrates it by using six vivid metaphors. The first three are already favourite images with Paul – the soldier, the athlete and the farmer. He has made use of them several times in former letters to illustrate a wide variety of truths. Here they all emphasize that Timothy's work will be strenuous, involving both labour and suffering.

2. Metaphor I: the dedicated soldier (2:3–4)

Paul's prison experiences had given him ample opportunity to watch Roman soldiers and to meditate on the parallels between the soldier and the Christian. In earlier letters he has referred to the warfare with rulers and authorities in which the Christian soldier is engaged, the armour which we must put on and the weapons which we must use (Eph. 6:10ff.; 1 Tim. 1:18; 6:12; 2 Cor. 6:7; 10:3–5; cf. Rom. 6:13–14). But here the *good soldier of Christ Jesus* is so called because he or she is a dedicated person who shows that dedication in a willingness both to suffer and to concentrate.

Soldiers on active service do not expect a safe or easy time. They take hardship, risk and suffering as a matter of course. These things are part and parcel of a soldier's calling. As Tertullian put it in his *Address to Martyrs*: 'No soldier comes to the war surrounded by luxuries, nor goes into action from a comfortable bedroom, but from the makeshift and narrow tent, where every kind of hardness and severity and unpleasantness is to be found.'[3] Similarly, the Christian should not expect an easy time. If we are loyal to the gospel, we are sure to experience opposition and ridicule. We must *join . . . in suffering* with our comrades-in-arms.

The soldier must be willing to concentrate as well as to suffer. When on active service no soldier 'gets himself entangled in business' (JBP). On the contrary, soldiers free themselves from civilian affairs in order to give themselves to soldiering and so satisfy their commanding officers. As E. K. Simpson expresses it, 'the spectacle of military discipline furnished a grand lesson of wholeheartedness'.[4] So in the Second World War people

---

[3] *Address to Martyrs*, chapter 2, para. 3. Alfred Plummer's translation, p. 346.
[4] Simpson, p. 131.

frequently said to each other with a wry smile, 'There's a war on' – a watchword sufficient to justify any austerity, self-denial or abstention from innocent activities because of the current emergency.

The Christian, who is intended to live in the world and not contract out of it, cannot of course avoid ordinary duties at home, at work and in the community. Indeed as Christians we should be outstandingly conscientious in doing and not dodging them. Nor should we forget, as Paul reminded Timothy in his first letter, either that 'everything God created is good, and nothing is to be rejected if it is received with thanksgiving', or that 'God . . . richly provides us with everything for our enjoyment' (1 Tim. 4:4; 6:17). So what is forbidden the *good soldier of Jesus Christ* is not all 'secular' activities, but rather 'entanglements' which, though they may be perfectly innocent in themselves, may hinder us from fighting Christ's battles. This counsel applies especially to Christian ministers or pastors. They are called to devote themselves to teaching and tending Christ's flock, and there are other Scriptures besides this one to say that if possible they should not have the additional burden of having to get their living in some 'secular' employment.

It is true that the apostle himself had often earned his keep by his tent-making. Yet he made it plain that in his case the reason was personal and exceptional, namely to offer the gospel 'free of charge' and 'put up with anything rather than hinder the gospel of Christ' (1 Cor. 9:18, 12). He still asserted the principle for himself and for every minister, by command of the Lord, that 'those who preach the gospel should receive their living from the gospel' (1 Cor. 9:14). Indeed, he clearly expected this to be the general rule. And this needs to be remembered in our day when 'auxiliary', 'supplementary' and 'part-time' ministries are increasing, in which pastors continue their trade or profession and exercise their ministry in their spare time. Such ministries can hardly be said to go against Scripture. Yet they are difficult to reconcile with the apostle's ruling to avoid entanglements.

The application of this verse is wider than to pastors, however. All Christians are in some degree soldiers of Christ, even if they are as timid as Timothy. For, whatever our temperament, we cannot avoid the Christian conflict. And if we are to be good soldiers of Jesus Christ, we must be dedicated to the battle, committing ourselves to a life of discipline and suffering, and avoiding whatever may 'entangle' us and so distract us from it.

3. Metaphor II: the law-abiding athlete (2:5)

Paul now turns from the image of the Roman soldier to that of the competitor in the Greek games. In no athletic contest of the ancient world (any more than of the modern) was a competitor giving a random display of strength or skill. Every sport had its rules, always for the contest itself and sometimes for the preparatory training as well. Every event had its prize also, and the prizes awarded at the Greek games were evergreen wreaths, not gold medals or silver trophies. But no athletes, however brilliant, were 'crowned' unless they had competed *according to the rules.* 'No rules, no wreath' was the order of the day.

The Christian life is regularly pictured in the New Testament as a race, not in the sense that we are competing against each other, but in other ways: in the strenuous self-discipline of training (1 Cor. 9:24–27), in laying aside every hindrance (Heb. 12:1–2), and here, in keeping the rules.

We are to run the Christian race *nomimōs*, 'lawfully'. In spite of the strange teaching of those who insist that the category of law has been abolished by Christ, the Christian is under obligation to live 'lawfully', to keep the rules, to obey God's moral laws. True, we are not 'under law' as a way of salvation, to commend ourselves to God, but we are to use it as a guide to behaviour. So far from abolishing his law God first sent his Son to die for us 'in order that the righteous requirement of the law might be fully met in us', and now sends his Spirit to live in us and to write his law in our hearts (Rom. 8:3–4; Jer. 31:33)! Further, there is no crown otherwise, not, of course, because our law-abiding could ever justify us, but rather because without it we give evidence that we have never been justified.

The context requires that competing *according to the rules* has a wider application than to our moral conduct, however. Paul is describing Christian service, not just Christian life. He seems to be saying that rewards for service depend on faithfulness. Christian teachers must teach the truth, building with solid materials on the foundation of Christ, if their work is to endure and not be burned up (cf. 1 Cor. 3:10–15). So Timothy must faithfully pass on the deposit to reliable people. Only if, like Paul, he perseveres to the end, so that he too fights the good fight, finishes the race and keeps the faith, can he expect on the last day to receive that most coveted of all wreaths, 'the crown of righteousness' (2 Tim. 4:7–8).

4. Metaphor III: the hardworking farmer (2:6)

If athletes must play fair, farmers must work hard. They 'toil' at their job, as the verb indicates. Hard work is indeed indispensable to good farming. This is particularly so in lower-income countries before mechanization arrives. In such circumstances successful farming depends as much on sweat as on skill. However poor the soil, harsh the weather, or unwilling the farmers, they must keep at their work. Having put their hand to the plough, they must not look back. Bishop Moule writes of 'the strenuous and prosaic toil' of the farmer. Unlike the soldier and the athlete, the farmer's life is 'totally devoid of excitement, remote from all glamour of peril and of applause'.[5]

Yet the first share of the crops goes to the hardworking farmers. They deserve it. Their good yield is due as much to their toil and perseverance as to anything else. That is why lazy individuals never make good farmers, as the book of Proverbs insists. They always lose their harvest, either because they are asleep when they ought to be reaping, or because they were too lazy to plough the previous autumn, or because they have allowed their fields to become overgrown with nettles and thorns (Prov. 10:5; 20:4; 24:30–31).

To what kind of harvest is the apostle referring? Two applications are more obviously biblical than others.

First, holiness is a harvest. True, it is 'the fruit [or 'harvest'] of the Spirit', in that the Spirit is himself the chief farmer who produces a good crop of Christian qualities in the believer's life. But we have our part to play. We are to 'live by the Spirit' and 'sow to please the Spirit' (Gal. 5:16; 6:8), following his promptings and disciplining ourselves, if we would reap the harvest of holiness. Many Christians are surprised that they are not noticeably growing in holiness. Is it that we are neglecting to cultivate the field of our character? 'A man reaps what he sows' (Gal. 6:7). As Bishop Ryle emphasizes again and again in his great book entitled *Holiness*, there are 'no gains without pains'. For example:

> I will never shrink from declaring my belief that there are no 'spiritual gains without pains'. I should as soon expect a farmer to prosper in business who contented himself with sowing his fields and never looking

---

[5] Moule, p. 77.

at them till harvest, as expect a believer to attain much holiness who was not diligent about his Bible-reading, his prayers, and the use of his Sundays. Our God is a God who works by means, and He will never bless the soul of that man who pretends to be so high and spiritual that he can get on without them.[6]

As Paul puts it here, it is *the hardworking farmer* who has the first share of the crop. For holiness is a harvest.

Second, the winning of converts is a harvest too. 'The harvest is plentiful,' Jesus said, referring to the many who are waiting to hear and receive the gospel (Matt. 9:37; cf. John 4:35; Rom. 1:13). Now in this harvest it is of course 'God who makes things grow' (1 Cor. 3:6–7). But again we have no liberty to be idle. Further, both the sowing of the good seed of God's word and the reaping of the harvest are hard work, especially when the labourers are few. Souls are won for Christ only with great effort: not by the slick, automatic application of a formula, but by tears and sweat and pain, especially in prayer and in sacrificial personal friendship. Again, it is *the hardworking farmer* who can expect good results.

This notion that Christian service is hard work is so unpopular in some relaxed Christian circles today that I feel the need to underline it. I have already mentioned that the verb signifies to 'toil'. Arndt and Gingrich say that it means first of all to 'become weary, tired' and so to 'work hard, toil, strive, struggle'. Both the noun (*kopos*) and the verb (*kopiaō*) were favourite words with Paul, and it may be healthy for us to see what strong exertion he believed to be necessary in Christian service.

It goes without saying that the word can be used of manual labour, and Paul applied it to his tent-making. 'We work hard', he could write, 'with our own hands' (1 Cor. 4:12; cf. Eph. 4:28; 1 Thess. 4:11). But in his view spiritual work involved exertion too. He was quick to recognize thoroughness in others and sent special greetings at the end of his Roman letter to 'Mary, who worked very hard for you' and to 'my dear friend Persis, another woman who has worked very hard in the Lord' (Rom. 16:6, 12b). Not that Paul expected more of others than he was prepared to give himself. His exertions for the gospel were phenomenal. He could write of 'hard work, sleepless nights and hunger' because, like his Master before him, he was often too busy to sleep or to eat, and could claim in respect of

---

[6] *Holiness* by J. C. Ryle (James Clarke, 1952), p. 21.

the other apostles, 'I worked harder than all of them' (2 Cor. 6:5; 1 Cor. 15:10; cf. Gal. 4:11; Phil. 2:16). If we were to press him about the nature of this toil, I think he would reply in terms of those two apostolic priorities 'prayer and the ministry of the word' (Acts 6:4). For he referred in his first letter to Timothy to those elders 'whose work is preaching and teaching' (1 Tim. 5:17), and described to the Colossians how 'I strenuously contend with all the energy Christ so powerfully works in me' (Col. 1:29–2:1; cf. 1 Tim. 4:10) in a context which seems to refer to the prayer-battle in which he was engaged on their behalf.

The blessing of God rested upon the ministry of the apostle Paul in quite exceptional measure. No doubt many explanations of this could be given. But I find myself wondering if we attribute it sufficiently to the zeal and zest, the almost obsessional devotion, with which he gave himself to the work. He gave and did not count the cost; he fought and did not heed the wounds; he toiled and did not seek for rest; he laboured and asked for no reward except the joy of doing his Lord's will. And God prospered his efforts. Again, it is *the hardworking farmer* who gets a good crop.

So far, then, we have looked at the first three metaphors with which Paul illustrates the duties of the Christian worker. By them he has isolated three aspects of wholeheartedness which should be found in Timothy, and in all those who like Timothy seek to pass on to others 'the good deposit' they have themselves received: the dedication of a good soldier, the law-abiding obedience of a good athlete and the painstaking labour of a good farmer. Without these we cannot expect results. There will be no victory for soldiers unless they give themselves to their soldiering, no wreath for athletes unless they keep the rules, and no harvest for farmers unless they toil at their farming.

5. The way to understanding (2:7)

This verse concludes the first paragraph of the chapter. There is an important biblical balance here. If Timothy is to know and understand the truth, not least as expressed in the illustrations Paul has just given, two processes will be necessary, the one human and the other divine. Timothy himself must *reflect on* the apostle's teaching, listening to it carefully and applying his mind to it. For then the Lord will grant him understanding in everything. What Paul here expresses is a promise, and not merely a wish.

There are at least two important implications of this combination of human study and divine illumination for anybody who wants to inherit the promised gift of understanding from the Lord.

First, if we are to receive understanding from the Lord, we must consider what *the apostle* is saying. This is a good example of Paul's self-conscious apostolic authority. He commands Timothy to ponder his teaching and promises that the Lord will grant him *insight into all this* if he does so. He sees nothing strange about claiming that his teaching as an apostle deserves careful study, or that it can be interpreted by the Lord alone, or that this is the way for Timothy to grow in understanding. It is clear evidence that Paul believed his teaching to be not his own but the Lord's. Indeed, in the following verses, almost imperceptibly, he equates 'my gospel' (8) with 'God's word' (9).

Second, if we are to receive insight from the Lord, we must *reflect on* what the apostle is saying. Some Christians never get down to any serious Bible study. The reason may of course be that they are simply too lazy. Alternatively, it may be 'spiritual' (though I fear I would have to call it 'pseudo-spiritual'), namely that they believe understanding will come to them from the Holy Spirit and not from their own studies (which is a totally false contrast). So all they do is skim through some Bible verses in a haphazard and random fashion, hoping (and even praying) that the Holy Spirit will show them what it all means. But they do not obey the apostle's command, *Reflect on what I am saying.*

Others are very good at Bible study. They are 'hardworking farmers', as it were. They use their minds and grapple with the text of Scripture. They compare versions, consult concordances and pore over commentaries. But they forget that it is the Lord alone who imparts understanding, and that he imparts it as a gift.

So we must not divorce what God has joined together. For the understanding of Scripture a balanced combination of thought and prayer is essential. We must do the reflecting, and the Lord will do the giving of insight.

6. Suffering a condition of blessing (2:8–13)

We come now to a new paragraph before the apostle introduces three more pictures to illustrate the role of the Christian worker. So far we may summarize his theme by the epigram 'nothing that is easy is ever worth while', or rather the reverse, 'nothing that is worth while is ever easy'. No soldier, athlete or farmer expects results without labour or suffering. Here Paul continues the same theme. But having illustrated it by metaphor, he goes on to back it up from experience – the experience first of Christ (8), then of himself as an apostle (9–10) and lastly of all Christian believers (11–13).

a. The experience of Christ (2:8)

The command to *remember Jesus Christ* at first sight seems extraordinary. How could Timothy ever forget him? Yet the human memory is notoriously unreliable: it is possible to forget even one's own name! The epitaph over Israel's grave was 'they soon forgot', and it was to overcome our forgetfulness of Christ crucified that he deliberately instituted his supper as a feast of remembrance, a fragrant 'forget-me-not'. Even so the church has often forgotten Jesus Christ, absorbing itself instead now in barren theological debate, now in purely humanitarian activity, now in its own petty, parochial business.

How and why, then, are we to remember Christ? Essentially because he is the gospel, the heart of the good deposit. Indeed, Paul expresses it, he is the heart of *my gospel*, the gospel 'not invented by me but entrusted to me',[7] like 'my deposit' (1:12). So then, if Timothy is to guard the deposit, and to hand it on faithfully to others, he must *remember Jesus Christ . . . This is my gospel*.

In particular, Christ is to be remembered as the one who is both *raised from the dead* and *descended from David*. As we meditate on these two expressions, it is remarkable how full an account of the gospel they give. The birth, death, resurrection and ascension of Jesus are all implied by them. And these remind us both of his divine–human person and of his saving work.

First, his person. The words *descended from David* imply his humanity, for they speak of his earthly descent from David. The words *raised from the dead* imply his divinity, for he was powerfully shown to be God's Son by his resurrection from the dead.[8]

Second, his work. The phrase *raised from the dead* indicates that he died for our sins and was raised to prove the effectiveness of his sin-bearing

---

[7] Lock, p. 95.

[8] Rom. 1:4. Note that in Rom. 1:3 Jesus is also described as 'according to the flesh . . . a descendant of David' (NIV margin).

sacrifice. The phrase *descended from David* indicates that he has established his kingdom as great David's greater Son (cf. Luke 1:32–33). Taken together, the two phrases may be seen as referring to his double role as Saviour and King.

There is another reason why Timothy must *remember Jesus Christ, raised from the dead, descended from David.* It is not just because these facts make up the gospel which Timothy must preach, but because they also illustrate, from Jesus Christ's own experience, the principle that death is the gateway to life, and suffering the path to glory. For he who died rose from the dead, and he who was born in lowliness as David's seed is now reigning in glory on David's throne. Both expressions set forth in embryonic form the contrast between humiliation and exaltation.

'So then, Timothy,' the apostle seems to be saying, 'when you are tempted to avoid pain, humiliation, suffering or death in your ministry, remember Jesus Christ and think again!'

b. The experience of the apostle Paul (2:9–10)

Paul is suffering for the gospel. He is having to endure the painful indignity of wearing chains 'like a common criminal' (NEB) – the only other occurrence of the word in the New Testament is of the criminals crucified with Jesus (Luke 23:32–33) – although he is a Roman citizen and an innocent man. But, though he is chained, God's word is not. Even he himself at his first defence had been given the opportunity and the strength fully to proclaim God's word to the court, as he will later explain to Timothy in greater detail (4:16–17). In addition, God's word could spread (was spreading) through many others, and in particular Timothy must share increasingly in this work.

The relation between Paul's sufferings and the effectiveness of the gospel is not just one of contrast, however: *I am . . . chained . . . God's word is not.* It is actually one of cause and effect: *Therefore I endure everything for the sake of the elect, that they too may obtain . . . salvation.* We notice in passing that the doctrine of election does not do away with the need for preaching. On the contrary, it makes it essential. For Paul preaches and suffers for it (literally) 'in order that' they *may obtain the salvation that is in Christ Jesus, with eternal glory.* The elect obtain salvation in Christ not apart from the preaching of Christ, but by means of it.

Further, it is not just the preaching but also the resultant suffering which is the means of the elect's salvation. Paul's statement that in some sense the salvation of others is secured by his sufferings may at first astonish us. Yet it is so. Not of course that his sufferings have any redemptive value like Christ's, but that the elect are saved through the gospel and that he could not preach the gospel without suffering for it. It is another case of 'glory through suffering', the *eternal glory* of the elect through the sufferings endured by the apostle.

c. Our common Christian experience (2:11–13)

Paul now quotes a current saying or fragment of an early Christian hymn which he pronounces reliable.[9] It consists of two pairs of sayings which are general axioms of Christian life and experience. They apply equally to all believers. The first pair relates to those who remain true and endure, the second pair to those who become false and faithless.

> *If we died with him,*
> > *we will also live with him;*
> *if we endure,*
> > *we will also reign with him.*
> (11b–12a)

The death with Christ which is here mentioned must refer, according to the context, not to our death to *sin* through union with Christ in his death, but rather to our death to *self* and to *safety*, as we take up the cross and follow Christ. Paul describes the former in Romans 6:3 ('don't you know that all of us who were baptised into Christ Jesus were baptised into his death?'); the latter he expresses both in 1 Corinthians 15:31 ('I face death every day') and in 2 Corinthians 4:10 ('We always carry around in our body the death of Jesus'). That this is the meaning in the hymn fragments seems plain from the fact that to have *died with* Christ and to *endure* are parallel expressions.

So the Christian life is pictured as a life of dying, a life of enduring. Only if we share Christ's death on earth shall we share his life in heaven. Only if we share his sufferings and endure shall we share his reign in the world to come. For the road to life is death, and the road to glory, suffering (cf. Rom. 8:17; 2 Cor. 4:17).

---

[9] There are four similar quotations in the Pastorals introduced by the formula 'the saying is sure' (NIV 'here is a trustworthy saying'), namely in 1 Tim. 1:15; 3:1; 4:9; and Titus 3:8.

> If we disown him,
>   he will also disown us;
> if we are faithless,
>   he remains faithful,
>   for he cannot disown himself.
> (12b–13)

This other pair of sayings imagines the dreadful possibility of our disowning Christ and proving faithless. The first phrase *if we disown him, he will also disown us* seems to be an echo of our Lord's own warning: 'whoever disowns me before others, I will disown before my Father in heaven' (Matt. 10:33).

What, then, of the second phrase, *if we are faithless, he remains faithful*? It has often been taken as a comforting assurance that, even if we turn away from Christ, he will not turn away from us, for he will never be faithless as we are. And it is true, of course, that God never shows the inconsistency or the faithlessness of human beings. Yet the logic of the Christian hymn, with its two pairs of balancing sayings, really demands a different interpretation. *If we disown him* and *if we are faithless* are parallels, which requires that *he will also disown us* and *he remains faithful* be parallels also. In this case his 'faithfulness' when we are faithless will be faithfulness to his warnings. As William Hendriksen puts it: 'Faithfulness on his part means carrying out his threats . . . as well as his promises.'[10] So he will disown us, as the earlier saying asserts. Indeed, if he did not disown us (in faithfulness to his plain warnings), he would then disown himself. But one thing is certain about God beyond any doubt or uncertainty whatever, and that is *he cannot disown himself.*

The idea that there may be something which God *cannot* do is entirely foreign to some people. Can he not do anything and everything? Are not all things possible to him? Is he not all-powerful? Yes, but God's omnipotence needs to be understood. God is not a dictatorial tyrant that he should exercise his power indiscriminately and do absolutely anything whatsoever. God's omnipotence is the freedom and the power to do absolutely anything he chooses to do. But he chooses only to do good, only to work according to the perfection of his character and will. God can do everything consistent with being himself. The one and only thing he cannot do, because he will not, is to disown himself or act contrary to

---

[10] Hendriksen, p. 260.

himself. So God remains for ever himself, the same God of mercy and of justice, fulfilling his promises (whether of blessing or of judgment), giving us life if we die with Christ and a kingdom if we endure, but disowning us if we disown him, just as he warned, because he cannot disown himself.

Looking back over the first half of this chapter (1–13), the apostle Paul seems to have been hammering home a single lesson. From secular analogy (soldiers, athletes, farmers) and from spiritual experience (Christ's, his own, every Christian's) he has been insisting that blessing comes through pain, fruit through toil, life through death, and glory through suffering. It is an unchanging law of Christian life and service.

So why should we expect things to be easy for us or promise an easy time to others? Neither human wisdom nor divine revelation gives us such an expectation. Why, then, do we deceive ourselves and others? The truth is the reverse, namely 'no pains, no gains' or 'no cross, no crown'.

It is this principle which took Jesus Christ through a lowly birth and a shameful death to his glorious resurrection and heavenly reign. It is this principle which had brought Paul his chains and prison cell, in order that the elect might obtain salvation and glory. It is the same principle which makes the soldier willing to endure hardship, the athlete discipline and the farmer toil. It would be ridiculous, therefore, to expect our Christian life and service to cost us nothing.

In the second part of 2 Timothy 2 (14–26), Paul continues his vivid portrayal of Timothy in his role of teaching and transmitting the faith, and therefore by derivation of every Christian minister, teacher or worker. He now uses three more pictures – the 'worker who does not need to be ashamed' (15), the 'instruments for special purposes' (21) and 'the Lord's servant' (24). Each adds a further feature to the portrait.

7. Metaphor IV: the unashamed worker (2:14–19)

We will leave verse 14 aside for the moment and proceed straight to verse 15. Several facts are immediately evident from this exhortation to Timothy to aim to be an unashamed worker.

First, the kind of work Christian workers do is teaching. They are called to handle *the word of truth*.

Second, there are two kinds of workers. On the one hand, there are those who are *approved*, 'tried and true' (AG), who having been tested like coins or metals and passed the test are recognized as 'sterling';[11] on the other hand, there are those who are not approved, because they fail the test. The former group do *not need to be ashamed*, while the latter ought to be deeply ashamed of themselves.

Third, the difference between these two categories concerns their handling or treatment of *the word of truth*, the good deposit.

So Paul sets these two kinds of teachers in contrast, and supplies an example of each. Timothy (15) is to be a good worker, approved and not ashamed. Hymenaeus and Philetus (17), however, are bad workers who have forfeited God's approval (whatever approval they may have obtained from other people) and have every reason to be ashamed.

Further, the work of these good and bad workers is summed up in significant verbs. The good worker 'cuts straight' (15, literally) the word of truth; the bad worker 'swerves' (18) or departs from the truth. We must look at these more fully and separately.

a. The good worker

The verb in verse 15 (*orthotomeō*), translated *correctly handles*, means literally to 'cut straight'. It is a very unusual word and occurs three times only in biblical Greek, once in the New Testament (this verse) and twice in the book of Proverbs, where in 3:6 we read 'He will make your paths straight', and in 11:5, 'The righteousness of the blameless makes their paths straight.'

How, then, is *the word of truth* being pictured that Timothy is commanded to make or cut it straight? Not as a sacrificial victim to be cut into pieces, as some ancient commentators thought; nor as a loaf, so that 'Paul assigns to teachers the duty of carving or dividing the Word, like a father dividing the bread into small pieces to feed the children';[12] nor as a ribbon to be cut into strips, or a plot into allotments, as some more recent dispensationalists teach; nor even, I think, as a stone which masons cut to fit into a building, as C. K. Barrett suggests;[13] but rather as a road or path or – to be more modern – as a motorway or freeway needs to be cut straight through the countryside. Thus, Arndt and Gingrich define the verb as meaning to '"cut a path in a straight direction" or "cut

---

[11] Simpson, p. 136.
[12] Calvin, p. 313.
[13] Barrett, p. 105.

a road across country (that is forested or otherwise difficult to pass through) in a straight direction", so that the traveller may go directly to his destination'. Or, possibly, the metaphor may be taken rather from ploughing than from road-making, so that the NEB, following Chrysostom, renders it 'driving a straight furrow in your proclamation of the truth'.

The word of truth is the apostolic faith which Timothy has received from Paul and is to communicate to others. For us it is, quite simply, Scripture. To 'cut it straight' or 'make it a straight path' is to be accurate on the one hand and plain on the other in our exposition. Apparently Sophocles used the word for 'to expound soundly' (MM). Thus good workers are true to Scripture. They do not fabricate it.[14] Nor do they try to confuse people, like Elymas the sorcerer, by 'perverting the right ways of the Lord' (Acts 13:10). On the contrary, they handle the word with such meticulous care that they both stay on the path themselves, keeping to the highway and avoiding the side streets, and make it easy for others to follow.

b. The bad worker

The metaphor Paul employs to describe the bad worker is taken neither from civil engineering nor from agriculture, but from archery. So now the truth is likened not to a road being built or a furrow being ploughed, but to a target being shot at. The verb (18) is *astocheō*, which comes from *stochos*, a 'target', and means to 'miss the mark' and so to 'deviate' from something. It occurs three times in the pastoral epistles: 'Some have departed from these [a pure heart, a good conscience and a sincere faith] and have turned to meaningless talk' (1 Tim. 1:6); '. . . what is falsely called knowledge, which some have professed and in so doing have departed from the faith' (1 Tim. 6:21); *who have departed from the truth*, or, as in the NEB, 'shot wide of the truth' (2 Tim. 2:18).

We are now in a position to grasp the alternative which Paul sets before all Christian teachers entrusted with the word of truth, and which determines whether they will be good or bad workers.

The word of truth is a target. As we shoot at this target, we will either hit it or miss it.

---

[14] Cf. 2 Cor. 2:17. It is significant that the noun *orthotomia* was used by both Clement of Alexandria and Eusebius for 'orthodoxy'.

The word of truth is a road. As we cut this road through the forest, we will make it either straight or crooked.

As a result of what we do – that is, how we teach – others are bound to be affected, for better or for worse. If we cut the road straight, people will be able to follow and so keep in the way. If, on the other hand, we miss the mark, the attention of the spectators will be distracted from the target and their eyes will follow the arrow however widely astray it has gone.

Paul warns Timothy here of this grave danger. There were some in Asia who were teaching serious error. Instead of preaching Paul's gospel which included 'Jesus Christ, raised from the dead' (8), the promise and pattern of his people's resurrection, they were saying *that the resurrection has already taken place* (18). Of course, in one sense it has, in that Christ has risen and his people have already risen with him. Yet the resurrection of the body lies still in the future. The false teachers, however, were denying any bodily resurrection to come (cf. Acts 17:32; 1 Cor. 15:12). They were perhaps early Gnostics to whom the body was an evil nuisance and the concept of any bodily resurrection was therefore as unthinkable as it was undesirable. So they 'spiritualized' it as a release from the flesh through *gnōsis* ('knowledge'), or by asserting that the promise of resurrection had been entirely fulfilled when by faith and baptism we were raised with Christ. Similarly today some 'demythologize' the resurrection and speak only of faith rising in the Christian's heart.

Such heretics were substituting for *the word of truth* what Paul calls *quarrelling about words* (14). The verb he employs here (*logomacheō*) occurs nowhere else in the New Testament, although the noun *logomachia*, 'word-battle' (AG), is found in 1 Timothy 6:4 and some manuscripts of Titus 3:9. He seems to be referring to something 'like the hair-splittings of the schoolmen'[15] in the Middle Ages. Elsewhere he calls it *godless chatter* (16, *kenophōnia*, or 'empty talk').[16]

Paul's instruction to Timothy about such bad workers or false teachers is to *avoid* them: *Warn them before God against quarrelling about words; it is of no value, and only ruins those who listen* (14). *Avoid godless chatter, because those who indulge in it will become more and more ungodly. Their teaching will spread like gangrene* (16–17a).

---

[15] Simpson, p. 136.
[16] The only other occurrence of this word is in 1 Tim. 6:20.

The damage caused by such false teaching is double. It is both 'godless' and 'gangrenous'. That is, in the first place, it leads people away from God. What verse 16 literally says is that those who hold such teaching 'advance into more and more ungodliness'. It is hardly an 'advance', however. As Patrick Fairbairn comments,[17] it is 'a forward movement in the wrong direction'. In the second place, it spreads its infection in the community. Paul reiterates this three times for emphasis: *It is of no value, and only ruins those who listen* (14b); 'False teachings are as dangerous as blood-poisoning to the body, and spread like sepsis from a wound' (17, JBP); *they destroy the faith of some* (18b).

These two tendencies of heresy are most revealing. We would be wise to ask ourselves regarding every kind of teaching both what its attitude is towards God and what effect it has upon other people. There is invariably something about error which is dishonouring to God and damaging to people. The truth, on the other hand, always honours God, promoting godliness (cf. Titus 1:1), and always edifies its hearers. Instead of causing a *katastrophē* (14), upsetting them or turning them upside down, it builds them up in faith, love and holiness.

Although people's faith can be destroyed (18b), the foundation of God remains secure (19). This is the true church which he is building. It has a twofold 'seal' or *inscription*. The first is secret and invisible, namely *The Lord knows those who are his*, and will therefore keep them safe for ever. The second is public and visible, namely *Everyone who confesses the name of the Lord must turn away from wickedness*, and so prove that they belong to the Lord by their holiness. The reference is probably to the Old Testament story of the rebellion of Korah, Dathan and Abiram, from which incident both quotations come (Num. 16:5, 26). Ultimately, Paul is saying, it is only the Lord who knows and recognizes his own people, and can tell the true from the false, for only he sees the heart. But though we cannot see the heart, we can see the life, which is the one reliable evidence of the heart's condition, and is apparent to all. Both 'seals' are essential, however – the divine and the human, the unseen and the seen. Together they bear witness to *God's solid foundation*, his true church.

It is doubtless the reference to the necessity of departing from evil which leads Paul to the next metaphor.

---

[17] Fairbairn, p. 345.

8. Metaphor V: the clean article (2:20–22)

The picture which the apostle is painting is clear. Every house is equipped with articles or utensils of different kinds, pots and pans and dishes, and so on. In a *large house* or stately mansion these are many and varied. They may be divided approximately into two groups. There are the *articles ... of gold and silver*, which are *for special purposes*, and in particular for the personal service of the master of the house. There are also articles *of wood and clay*, which, apart from being of cheaper quality in themselves, are reserved for *common use* in the kitchen and the scullery.

What is the apostle referring to by this metaphor? There can be little doubt that the *large house* is God's house, the visible or professing church. But what are the *articles*? The use of the term elsewhere in the New Testament suggests that they stand not simply for members of the church, but for the church's teachers. For example, Jesus had said to Ananias about the newly converted Saul of Tarsus: 'This man is my chosen instrument to proclaim my name to the Gentiles and their kings and to the people of Israel' (Acts 9:15). Years later Paul described himself and his co-workers by a similar image when he wrote: 'we have this treasure in jars of clay' (2 Cor. 4:7). In these verses 'instrument' and 'jars' translate the same Greek word (*skeuos*) that Paul is now using in his letter to Timothy (cf. 21, *instruments*). A *skeuos* was any kind of utensil. It is true that when he called himself a 'clay' jar he was applying the metaphor differently, for he was there emphasizing his physical infirmity, and not implying that he was fit only for common use. Nevertheless, the theme of service is prominent in each verse. As an 'instrument' Paul's function was to carry Christ's name before unbelievers, and in the clay jar he carried the treasure of the gospel, as a fragile pottery lamp carries the light.

From this usage I think we would be justified in concluding that the two sets of articles in the large house (gold and silver for special purposes, wood and clay for common) represent not genuine and spurious members of the church but true and false teachers in the church. Paul is still, in fact, referring to the two sets of teachers he has contrasted in the previous paragraph, the authentic like Timothy and the bogus like Hymenaeus and Philetus. The only difference is that he changes the metaphor from good and bad workers to special and common articles.

It would be difficult to exaggerate the privilege which the apostle here sets before Timothy in verse 21. Indeed he extends it to any and every

Christian minister or worker who will fulfil the condition, for his statement is couched in quite general terms: *those who cleanse themselves*. The privilege is described by simple yet beautiful expressions. They *will be instruments for special purposes*. This is then elaborated by three further expressions: *made holy* (permanently set apart), *useful* [or 'serviceable'] *to the Master* and *prepared to do any good work*. No higher honour could be imagined than to be an instrument in the hand of Jesus Christ, to be at his disposal for the furtherance of his purposes, to be available whenever wanted for his service.

The Master of the house lays down only one condition: the articles which he uses must be clean. His promise hinges on this. It is evident at once that some kind of self-purification is the essential condition of usefulness to Christ, but exactly what is it? The words *apo toutōn, from the latter* (plural), must refer back to the 'articles for common use' of the previous verse. In what sense, then, are we to purify ourselves from these? It cannot mean that we are to separate ourselves from all nominal church members whom we suspect of being bogus, and split from the visible church, for Jesus indicated in his parable that the weeds had been sown among the wheat and could not be successfully separated from them until the harvest. Besides, we have already seen that it is teachers rather than members who are indicated by the two sorts of articles. This fact and the context suggest, therefore, that we are to maintain our distance from the kinds of false teachers who, like Hymenaeus and Philetus, both deny some fundamental of the gospel and (according to 1 Tim. 1:19–20) have also violated their conscience and lapsed into some form of unrighteousness. But Paul's condition is more radical even than this. What we are to avoid is not so much contact with such people as their error and their evil. To cleanse ourselves from these is essentially to purge their falsehood from our minds and their wickedness from our hearts and lives. Purity, then – purity of doctrine and purity of life – is the essential condition of being serviceable to Christ.

That this is the correct interpretation is confirmed by the fact that the metaphor of the large house and its articles (20–21) is sandwiched in between two clear references to personal holiness: 'Everyone who confesses the name of the Lord must turn away from wickedness' (19) and 'Flee the evil desires of youth and pursue righteousness' (22). It is perfectly true that in his sovereign providence God has sometimes chosen to use impure vessels as the instruments both of his judgment and of his salvation. In Old Testament days he described pagan Assyria as 'the rod of my anger' with which he smote stubborn Israel, and which he then discarded (Isa. 10:5ff.). He also called the Babylonian king Nebuchadnezzar 'my servant' through whom he judged his people, and the Persian king Cyrus his 'shepherd' and his 'anointed' through whom he redeemed them (Jer. 25:9; 27:6; 43:10; and Isa. 44:28; 45:1). But these were exceptional cases; they were also national, rather than personal. The overwhelming emphasis of Scripture is that God chooses to use clean vessels, 'instruments of righteousness' (Rom. 6:13), for the fulfilment of his purposes. Certainly in Paul's appeal to Timothy he must cleanse himself if he is to be fit for the Master to use.

The apostle now explains what he means in an outspoken appeal which is both negative and positive. Negatively, Timothy is to *flee the evil desires of youth*. This is not to be understood exclusively as a reference to sexual lust, but to 'self-assertion as well as self-indulgence',[18] to selfish ambition, headstrong obstinacy, arrogance and indeed all the 'wayward impulses of youth' (NEB). Positively, Timothy is to *pursue* the four essential marks of a Christian – *righteousness, faith, love and peace* – and he is to aim for these in good company (maybe to compensate for the company he will have to avoid if he is to 'cleanse himself from what is common'), the company of *those who call on the Lord out of a pure heart*, that is, who share with Timothy the same hunger for righteousness and who cry to God with complete sincerity to satisfy their hunger.

As we listen to Paul's moral appeal, it is important not to miss the sharp contrast between its negative and positive aspects, and in particular between the two verbs *flee* and *pursue*. Both are strongly suggestive. *Pheugō* (*flee*) means literally to 'seek safety in flight' or 'escape' (AG). It is used literally of flight from physical danger, as when Moses fled from Pharaoh's wrath and the holy family from Herod's (Acts 7:29; Matt. 2:13). So too the hired hand flees from the wolf; and the Judean Christians, when in AD 70 Jerusalem was surrounded by the legions of Rome, were to flee to the mountains (John 10:12–13; Luke 21:21). In just the same way, when the verb is used figuratively, it denotes flight from spiritual danger. All sinners are urged to 'flee from the coming wrath' (Matt. 3:7). All Christians are commanded to flee from idolatry, from immorality, from the spirit of materialism and the love of money, and here from the evil desires of youth

---

[18] Lock, p. 101.

(1 Cor. 10:14; 6:18; 1 Tim. 6:11). True, we are also told to resist the devil, so that he may flee from us (Jas 4:7). But we are to recognize sin as something dangerous to the soul. We are not to come to terms with it, or even negotiate with it. We are not to linger in its presence like Lot in Sodom (Gen. 19:15–16). On the contrary, we are to get as far away from it as possible as quickly as possible. Like Joseph, when Potiphar's wife attempted to seduce him, we are to take to our heels and run (Gen. 39:12).

The verb *diōkō* (*pursue*) is the exact opposite. For if *pheugō* means to run away from, *diōkō* means to run after, to 'chase, in war or hunting' (LS). Its distinctive literal use in the New Testament (about thirty times) is of persecution. Paul himself uses it to describe his activities before his conversion: how he violently persecuted God's church (Gal. 1:13) and in his raging fury against the Christians even hounded them out of Jewish territory into foreign cities (Acts 26:11). Metaphorically, this verb is used to portray the Christian's pursuit of the will of God. Under the picture of a chariot race Paul describes himself as straining forward with eagerness, and adds 'I press on' and again 'I press on towards the goal' (Phil. 3:12, 14). In particular, the Christian is urged[19] to pursue moral righteousness with the same diligence with which the Jews pursued legal righteousness (Rom. 9:31). In other passages this righteousness or 'holiness' (Heb. 12:14) is broken up into its individual parts and supplemented with other virtues. Thus, we are to go in hot pursuit of *righteousness, faith, love and peace* (here) or 'righteousness, godliness, faith, love, endurance and gentleness' (1 Tim. 6:11); or simply 'love' (1 Cor. 14:1), and especially that love for strangers called 'hospitality' (Rom. 12:13) and the 'good' of others which love always seeks (1 Thess. 5:15); or simply 'peace', that all-inclusive grace, together with 'what leads to peace and to mutual edification' (Heb. 12:14a; 1 Pet. 3:11, quoting Ps. 34:14; Rom. 14:19). In all these verses the same verb *diōkō*, 'pursue', is used.

So, then, putting back together these two parts of Paul's appeal which we have studied separately, we are both to run away from spiritual danger and to run after spiritual good; both to flee from the one in order to escape it and to pursue the other in order to attain it. This double duty of Christians – negative and positive – is the consistent, repeated teaching of Scripture. Thus, we are to deny ourselves and to follow Christ. We are to put off what belongs to our old life and to put on what belongs to our new

---

[19] Here and in 1 Tim. 6:11.

life. We are to put to death our earthly desires and to set our minds on heavenly things. We are to crucify the flesh and to walk in the Spirit. It is the ruthless rejection of the one in combination with the relentless pursuit of the other which Scripture reveals to us as the secret of holiness. This is the only way we can hope to be fit for the Master's use. If the promise is to be inherited (they *will be instruments for special purposes*), the condition must be fulfilled (*those who cleanse themselves from the* articles for common use).

9. Metaphor VI: the Lord's servant (2:23–26)

The metaphor changes yet again. The instrument in the house becomes a slave in the household. The *skeuos* is transformed into a *doulos*. But before outlining the kind of behaviour appropriate for the Lord's servant, Paul sets the context in which he has to live and work. He returns to the 'quarrelling about words' of verse 14 and the 'godless chatter' of verse 16.

The word translated *arguments* (23) (*zētēsis*, a singular noun) is normally used in one of two senses. It means either an 'investigation', like the legal enquiry into charges against Paul which Festus told King Agrippa he was at a loss to know how to make (Acts 25:20), or a 'discussion', like the debate between the apostles and the Judaizers over circumcision (Acts 15:2, 7). If it is used here in the former sense, it will refer to some kind of philosophical investigation and could be translated 'speculation'. But if it is used in the latter sense, the reference will be to a 'controversy'.

The word occurs three times in the pastoral epistles, once in each letter (1 Tim. 6:4; 2 Tim. 2:23; Titus 3:9), or four times if the slightly stronger word *ekzētēsis* is added (1 Tim. 1:4). This latter word certainly seems to mean a 'useless speculation' (AG). In the context it is the fruit of a preoccupation with 'myths and endless genealogies'. At the end of the same letter, however, the word *zētēseis* (plural) is coupled with *logomachiai*, meaning 'word-battles', both of which are said to 'result in envy, strife, malicious talk, evil suspicions and constant friction' (1 Tim. 6:4–5a). So there the emphasis is rather upon heated controversy.

Perhaps there is no need to choose between the two meanings. They certainly appear to be combined in Titus 3:9, where Titus is told to avoid four things – 'controversies [*zētēseis*] and genealogies [the speculative idea again] and arguments [*ereis*] and quarrels [*machas*, 'battles'] about the law'. This last word is prominent in 2 Timothy 2 also, for in verse 23 Paul warns that *zētēseis produce quarrels* (*machas* again), and forbids people, in verse 14, *logomachein* (to quarrel about words; cf. 1 Tim. 6:4) or, in verse 24, *machesthai* (to quarrel or fight). Calvin's expression 'quarrelsome specu-lation'[20] neatly unites both emphases.

What, then, is being forbidden to Timothy, and through him to all the Lord's servants and ministers today? We cannot conclude that this is a ban on all controversy. For when the truth of the gospel was at stake Paul himself had been keen to engage in controversy, even to the extent of opposing the apostle Peter to his face in public (Gal. 2:11–14). Besides, in these very pastoral epistles he is urging Timothy and Titus to guard the sacred deposit of the truth and contend for it. Every Christian must in some sense 'fight the good fight of the faith' (1 Tim. 6:12; 2 Tim. 4:7), seeking to defend and preserve it. What is forbidden us is controversies which in themselves are *foolish and stupid* and in their effect *produce quarrels*. They are *foolish* or 'futile' (JB) because they are speculative. For the same reason they are *stupid* (*apaideutos*), literally 'uninstructed' or even 'undisciplined', because they go beyond Scripture and do not submit to the intellectual discipline which Scripture should impose upon us. They also inevitably *produce quarrels* because when people forsake revelation for speculation, they have no agreed authority and no impartial court of appeal. They lapse into pure subjectivism and so into profitless argument in which one person's opinion is as good (or bad) as another's. If only the church had heeded this warning! The combination of unbiblical speculations and uncharitable attacks has done great damage to the cause of Christ.

The fundamental characteristic of *the Lord's servant* is to be gentleness (25a). We have already seen that these 'servants' are called to a teaching ministry. They therefore need to be *able to teach* (*didaktikos*), endowed with a gift or skill in teaching. Their instruction will sometimes have to be negative as well as positive. That is to say, they are called not only to teach the truth to the people committed to their care, but also to correct error. They must not shrink from correcting their opponents. But in all their ministry, instructing and correcting alike, they will exhibit the same distinctive quality. They *must not be quarrelsome*. Instead, they will be *kind to everyone ... not resentful*, and will instruct *gently*. The first word, *kind* (*ēpios*), means 'mild' and is used by Paul to describe the attitude

---

20 Calvin, p. 312.

of 'a nursing mother' as she 'cares for her children' (1 Thess. 2:7). The second word, *not resentful* (*anexikakos*), means literally 'bearing evil without resentment' (AG) and so bearing with people's unkindness, patient towards their foolishness and tolerant of their foibles. The last word of the three, *gently* (*praütēs*), adds to the gentleness portrayed by the other two the notes of 'humility, courtesy, considerateness and meekness' (AG). Its opposite is to be brash, haughty and rude.

All this is the character which is fitting in *the Lord's servant* and, of course, deliberately reminds us of 'the servant of the Lord' portrayed in the 'servant songs' of Isaiah. That servant was a teacher, for the Lord God gave him 'a well-instructed tongue', and he used it wisely. He knew 'the word that sustains the weary'. So meek was he in his ministry that he would never shout or make a noise, and so sensitive that he would deal gently with people whose courage had been bruised and whose faith burned low. He would never break a bruised reed or snuff out a smouldering wick. And when people rose up in opposition to him he did not resist or retaliate. He gave his back to those who beat him, his cheeks to those who pulled out his beard, his face to those who spat upon him, and eventually allowed himself to be led like a sheep silent and unresisting to the slaughter (Isa. 50:4; 42:2–3; 50:6; 53:7). Such was Jesus of Nazareth, the supreme example of the Lord's servant, who described himself as 'gentle and humble in heart' (Matt. 11:29). And this same 'humility and gentleness of Christ' (2 Cor. 10:1) must characterize all who claim to be the Lord's servants today.

Moreover, if the Lord's servants enhance their Christian teaching with a Christian character, and if they are meek in their dealings with the wayward, instructing their opponents gently, lasting good may follow. God himself, through such a gentle ministry, may perform a conspicuous work of salvation.

We must observe carefully in verses 25b–26 how these opponents of apostolic truth are regarded. They are evidently sinful, for they need to repent, and also in error, for they need to be led to *a knowledge of the truth*. But most striking of all is that the evil and the error in which they are involved are both seen as symptoms of *the trap of the devil* from whom they need to be rescued. And further, important as is the part played by the gentle servant of the Lord in correcting them, it is God who 'grants' (*dōē*) them repentance, God who illumines their minds to acknowledge the truth, and God who liberates them from Satan's power.

The Greek expression *grant them repentance leading them to* [*eis*] *a knowledge of the truth* makes their knowledge of the truth the consequence of their repentance. It is a good example of the strong link which Scripture everywhere forges between the moral and the intellectual. Everybody knows that our belief determines our behaviour, but not everybody is so clear that our behaviour also determines our belief. Just as to violate our conscience leads to the shipwreck of our faith (1 Tim. 1:19), so to repent of our sin leads to a knowledge of the truth.

There is some uncertainty about the last phrase of verse 26, *who has taken them captive to do his will*. It is not clear whether the *one* who captures them and the one whose will they do relate to God or to the devil. Some commentators think that both refer to God and thus describe the divine capture which secures the people's escape from the devil. They are 'caught now by God and made subject to his will' (NEB margin). The verb *taken . . . captive* is *zōgreō* and means to 'capture alive' (AG). Its only other New Testament use is in Luke 5:10, where Jesus tells Peter the fisherman that in future he will 'fish for people'. Perhaps for this reason some commentators attribute the capture to the Lord's servant himself; for example, Lock: 'May it not even be that I shall be a fisher of men, and save them alive, and bring them back to do their true Master's will?'[21]

Others think that the captivity is the devil's, although the will is God's. In this case the people 'escape from the snare of the devil, after being captured by him, to do his [that is, God's] will' (RSV margin).

But most commentators take both as relating to the devil. In this case the phrase is simply enlarging on what is meant by *the trap* of Satan. In it 'the devil caught them and kept them enslaved' (JB). If this is correct, it enables us to see backstage in every Christian evangelistic and teaching ministry. Behind the scenes, invisible to those on the stage and in the audience, a spiritual battle is being fought out. The devil's grim activity is pictured graphically. He is likened to a hunter who captures his quarry alive in some clever trap. He also drugs or inebriates his captives, for the word used of their escape (*ananēphō*) means literally to 'become sober' or 'come to one's senses again' (AG) after a period of devilish intoxication. From such a captivity, in which people are both trapped and doped by the devil, only God can deliver them by giving them repentance leading them to know the truth. Yet he brings the rescue about through the human

---

[21] Lock, p. 98.

ministry of one of his servants, who avoids quarrelling and teaches with kindness, patience and gentleness.

Looking back over the chapter, we are now able to picture in our minds the composite portrait of the ideal Christian minister or worker which Paul has been painting with a variety of words and images. As good soldiers, law-abiding athletes and hardworking farmers, we must be utterly dedicated to our work. As unashamed workers we must be accurate and clear in our explanation of the gospel. As articles for special use we must be righteous in our character and conduct. And as the Lord's servants we must be courteous and gentle in our manner. Thus each metaphor concentrates on a particular characteristic which contributes to the portrait as a whole, and in fact lays down a condition of usefulness. Only if we give ourselves without reserve to our soldiering, running and farming can we expect results. Only if we cut the truth straight and do not swerve from it shall we be approved by God and have no need to be ashamed. Only if we purify ourselves from what is common, from all sin and error, shall we be articles for special use, of value to the Master of the house. Only if we are gentle and not quarrelsome, as the Lord's true servants, will God grant our opponents repentance, knowledge of the truth and deliverance from the devil.

Such is our heavy responsibility to labour and suffer for the gospel. No wonder the chapter began with a call to 'be strong in the grace that is in Christ Jesus'.

2 Timothy 3:1–17

3. The charge to continue in the gospel

As he lies in his cell, a prisoner of the Lord, Paul is still preoccupied with the future of the gospel. His mind dwells now on the evil of the times, now on the shyness of Timothy. Timothy is so weak, and the opposition so strong. It seems strange that such a man should be called in such a situation to contend for the truth. So the apostle begins with a vivid sketch of the contemporary scene, and against this background summons Timothy – in spite of the almost universal turning away from God and in spite of his own temperamental frailty – to continue faithful to what he has learned.

1. Facing terrible times (3:1–2a)

Why does Paul introduce this chapter with such an emphatic command to Timothy to *mark this*? After all, the existence of active opposition to the gospel is evident. Paul himself has been arrested, chained and imprisoned because of his own loyalty to it (1:11–12; 2:9). Everybody in Asia has shunned him, as Timothy is well aware (1:15). And earlier in the letter the apostle has urged his young friend not to be ashamed of the gospel but to take his share of suffering as Christ's good soldier; has reminded him that he must endure with Christ if he hopes one day to reign with him; and has warned him that behind the 'word-battles', 'godless chatter' and 'foolish and stupid arguments' spread by false teachers there lurks the evil figure of the devil himself (1:8; 2:3, 11–12, 14, 16, 23, 26). So why does the apostle tell Timothy to mark what he already knows? Surely because he wants to emphasize that opposition to the truth is not a passing situation, but a permanent characteristic of the age. Perhaps he fears that Timothy will be over-optimistic, hoping that if he lies low for a while, the storm will pass. But Paul gives him no such hope. We too should *mark this*, and be quite clear about the dangers and troubles which will affect us if we stand firm in the truth of the gospel.

Next, Paul refers to *the last days*. It may seem natural to apply this term to a future era, to the days immediately before the end when Christ returns. But biblical usage will not allow us to do this. For it is the conviction of the New Testament authors that the new age (promised in the Old Testament) arrived with Jesus Christ, and that therefore with his coming the old age had begun to pass away and the last days had dawned. So on the Day of Pentecost Peter quoted Joel's prophecy that 'in the last days' God would pour out his Spirit upon all people, and declared that this prophecy had now been fulfilled. 'This is what was spoken by the prophet Joel,' he said. In other words, 'the last days' to which the prophecy referred had come (Acts 2:14–17). Similarly, the letter to the Hebrews begins with an assertion that the God who had spoken of old to the ancestors through the prophets has 'in these last days' spoken to us through his Son (1:1–2). This being so, we are living in the last days. They were ushered in by Jesus Christ, God's Son.

What follows in 2 Timothy 3, therefore, is a description of the present, not the future. Paul describes the whole period elapsing between the first and second comings of Christ. 'Under *the last days* he includes the universal condition of the Christian Church.'[1] This not only follows from the way in which the expression 'the last days' is used in the New Testament. It is also clear from the fact that what Paul gives Timothy here is not predictions about some future time which he will not himself live to see, but instructions relating to his present ministry, including (for example) the command to 'have nothing to do with' certain people (5).[2] Timothy is already living in 'the last days' to which Paul is referring. And so are we. They may get worse in the future (13), but even now the times are bad and dangerous.

In these last days, Paul adds, *there will be terrible times*. What Timothy is to understand about the last days is not that they are uniformly,

---

[1] Calvin, p. 322.

[2] Similarly, the backsliders and the scoffers who belong to 'the last days' or the 'later times' and are referred to in 1 Tim. 4:1; 2 Pet. 3:3; and Jude 18 are regarded as already active when Paul, Peter and Jude were writing.

continuously evil, but that they will include 'perilous times' (AV). Church history confirms that this has been so. As the vessel of the Christian church put out to sea, it was not to expect a smooth, untroubled passage; it has been buffeted by storms and tempests and even hurricanes.

These seasons Paul denotes as *terrible times*. The Greek adjective *chalepos* means basically 'hard' or 'difficult', and implies either 'hard to bear' (for example, in the case of physical or mental pain) or 'hard to deal with, violent, dangerous' (AG), 'menacing'.[3] The word was used in classical Greek both of dangerous wild animals and of the raging sea. Its only other New Testament occurrence is in the story of the two demon-possessed men in the region of the Gadarenes who were as savage and untamed as wild beasts and whom Matthew describes as 'so violent [*chalepos*] that no one could pass that way' (Matt. 8:28). This gives us an idea of the kinds of seasons which the church must expect in the last days. They will be both painful and perilous, hard to endure and hard to cope with.

Paul goes on immediately to tell us why this is so: *People will be . . .* It is important to grasp that it is *people* who are responsible for the menacing seasons which the church has to bear – fallen people, evil people, people whose nature is perverted, whose behaviour is self-centred and godless, whose mind is hostile to God and his law (cf. Rom. 8:7), and who spread evil, heresy and dead religion in the church.

Before we study in detail Paul's characterization of these people, we need to absorb his words of introduction. First, we are living in the last days, he says; Christ brought them with him when he came. Second, these days will include seasons of danger and stress. Third, they will be the result of the activities of bad people. Fourth, we are to understand this, to be quite clear about it, and so to be prepared.

2. The evil people are described (3:2–9)

The rest of this first paragraph of chapter 3 is devoted to a thorough portrayal of these people. In particular, Paul describes their moral conduct (2–4), their religious observance (5) and their proselytizing zeal (6–9).

---

[3] Simpson, p. 143.

a. Their moral conduct (3:2–4)

In these three verses the apostle employs no fewer than nineteen expressions by which to describe the wicked people who are responsible for the 'terrible times'. It might perhaps be a little tedious to analyse the portrait too minutely and to define each term separately. But notice at once the first and the last phrases used. The first says that they are *lovers of themselves* (*philautoi*) and the last (4) that they are not, as they should be, *lovers of God* (*philotheoi*). Indeed four of the nineteen expressions are compounded with 'love' (*phil-*), suggesting that what is fundamentally wrong with these people is that their love is misdirected. Instead of being first and foremost *lovers of God*, they are *lovers of themselves*, *lovers of money* and *lovers of pleasure* (4).

In between these four come fifteen other expressions, which are almost entirely descriptive of the breakdown of people's relationships with one another.

The first three expand on the meaning of self-love. People who love themselves best become *boastful*, *proud* and *abusive*. The first word means 'braggarts' or 'swashbucklers' (*alazones*), and the second 'haughty' or 'disdainful' (*hyperēphanoi*), which leads naturally to the third, 'slanderous' (*blasphēmoi*), because inevitably those who have an exaggerated opinion of themselves look down with contempt upon others and speak evil of them.

The next five words may conveniently be grouped together. For they seem to refer to family life, and especially to the attitude which some young people adopt towards their parents. The Greek words are all negative in form and begin with the prefix *a-*, like our English words beginning un- or dis-, as if to stress the tragic absence of qualities which nature alone would lead one to expect. The first two are *disobedient to their parents*, whom Scripture says children are to honour and – at least before they come of age – obey; and *ungrateful*, devoid of even a basic appreciation. The next word is translated *unholy* (*anosioi*), for *hosios* normally means 'devout' or 'pious' towards God. But like the similar adjective *eusebēs* ('reverent') it was sometimes used in classical Greek of the respect due to parents. The context suggests that this may be the reference here. *Without love* (*astorgoi*) is rendered by the JBP 'utterly lacking in . . . normal human affections' and by the RSV in Romans 1:31 'heartless', because it is part of the natural, created order that parents and children should love each other. The last word of this group of five is *unforgiving* (*aspondoi*) and is translated by AG 'irreconcilable'. It describes a situation in which people (maybe the reference is still primarily to young people) are so much in revolt that they are not even willing to come to the conference table to negotiate. In an ideal society the relationship of children to their parents should be marked by obedience, gratitude, respect, affection and reasonableness. In 'times of stress' all five are lacking.

The remaining seven words of the catalogue are obviously wider than the family. The first is *slanderous* (*diaboloi*, literally 'devils'), translated 'backbiters' by E. K. Simpson and 'scandalmongers' in the NEB. They are guilty of the sin of speaking evil against others, especially behind their backs. They are also *without self-control* (*akrateis*) or 'ungovernable' (Simpson); *brutal* (*anēmeroi*) or 'untamed' (AG); and *not lovers of the good* (*aphilagathoi*) or 'strangers to all goodness' (NEB). Finally, they are *treacherous* (a word used in Luke 6:16 of the traitor Judas), *rash* (entirely thoughtless in word and deed) and *conceited* or 'puffed up' (indicating 'self-importance, bumptiousness'[4]). So we are back to the basic evil with which the hideous list began, namely pride.

And all this unsocial, antisocial behaviour – this disobedient, ungrateful, disrespectful, inhuman attitude to parents, together with this absence of restraint, loyalty, prudence and humility – is the inevitable consequence of a godless self-centredness. Archbishop Trench, commenting on the meaning of *philautos*, 'selfish', mentions an unnamed Puritan divine who 'likens the selfish man to the hedgehog which, rolling itself up in a ball, presents only sharp spines to those without, keeping at the same time all the soft and warm wool for itself within'.[5] If someone is 'boastful', 'proud' and 'conceited', that person will, of course, never sacrifice him- or herself to serve others. God's order, as plainly declared in his moral law, is that we love him first (with all our heart, soul, mind and strength), our neighbour next and ourselves last. If we reverse the order of the first and third, putting self first and God last, our neighbour in the middle is bound to suffer.

So the root of the trouble in *terrible times* is that people are 'utterly self-centred' (JBP), 'lovers of self' (*philautoi*), 'an Aristotelian term . . . for inordinate self-love'.[6]

---

[4] Simpson, p. 144.

[5] *Synonyms of the New Testament* by R. C. Trench (1854, 9th edition 1880), xciii, p. 329.

[6] Simpson, p. 143.

Only the gospel offers a radical solution to this problem. For only the gospel promises a new birth or new creation, which involves being turned inside out, from self to unself, a real reorientation of mind and behaviour, and which makes us essentially God-centred instead of self-centred. Then, when God is first and self is last, we love the world God loves and seek to give and serve like him.

b. Their religious observance (3:5)

It may be a shock to discover that people such as these, who lack the common decencies of civilized society let alone of God's law, can also be religious. But it is true. In the history of humanity, although this is a shameful thing to have to admit, religion and morality have been more often divorced than married. Certainly Scripture bears an unwavering testimony to this fact. The great ethical prophets of the seventh and eighth centuries BC raged against Israel and Judah on this score. Amos was the first, exposing the anomaly that in the reign of Jeroboam II there was a boom in religion and in injustice simultaneously. Israelite worshippers 'lie down beside every altar on garments taken in pledge', he cried; 'in the house of their god they drink wine taken as fines' (Amos 2:8). In other words, in the very performance of their religious duties they were making use of garments and wine to which they had no moral right. Their immorality had actually invaded their religious observance.

Isaiah condemned the same thing in Judah. Through him God addressed his people like this:

> Your New Moon feasts and your appointed festivals
> > I hate with all my being.
> They have become a burden to me;
> > I am weary of bearing them.
> When you spread out your hands in prayer,
> > I hide my eyes from you;
> even when you offer many prayers,
> > I am not listening.
>
> Your hands are full of blood!
>
> Wash and make yourselves clean.
> > Take your evil deeds out of my sight;
> > stop doing wrong.

Learn to do right; seek justice.
    Defend the oppressed.
Take up the cause of the fatherless;
    plead the case of the widow.
(Isa. 1:14–17)

The Lord Jesus had to utter a very similar complaint against the Pharisees, the ultra-religious people of his day: 'you clean the outside of the cup and dish, but inside they are full of greed and self-indulgence' (Matt. 23:25). That is, they were meticulous in ensuring the ceremonial purity of their vessels, while what they ate and drank from their clean vessels had been acquired by unclean greed and dishonesty.

Still the same problem was rife among the people Paul is describing. They preserved the outward *form of godliness* but were *denying its power* (5). They evidently attended the worship services of the church. They sang the hymns and songs, said the 'amen' to the prayers and put their money in the offering. They looked and sounded outstandingly pious. But it was *form* without *power*, outward show without inward reality, religion without morals, faith without works.

True religion combines form and power. It is not external form without power. Nor, on the other hand, does it emphasize moral power in such a way as to despise or dispense with proper external forms. It combines them. It encourages a worship which is essentially 'spiritual', arising from the heart, but which expresses itself through public, corporate services, and which also leads to moral behaviour. Otherwise, it is not only value-less; it is actually an abomination to the Lord.

No wonder Paul adds: *have nothing to do with such people.* Not that he was to avoid all contact with sinners, for Jesus himself had been 'the friend of tax collectors and sinners', and if Timothy were to avoid associating with them he would have to go right out of the world (cf. 1 Cor. 5:9–12). Paul means rather that within the church, for he has been giving a description of 'a kind of heathen Christianity',[7] Timothy was to have nothing to do with what might be called 'religious sinners'. Indeed, one could go further. Anybody whom the Church of England's old Book of Common Prayer terms 'an open and notorious evil liver' should be disciplined, and, if he or she remains unrepentant, excommunicated (cf. 1 Cor. 5:5, 13).

---

[7] Ellicott, p. 144.

c. Their proselytizing zeal (3:6–9)

It is indeed astonishing that the kinds of people the apostle has been describing, filled with godless self-love and malice, should not only profess religion, but include some who actively spread it. Yet such was the case.

It seems probable that their proselytizing zeal is portrayed as a military operation. The verb translated *gain control over* (*aichmalōtizō*) properly means to 'take prisoner in war', although AG add that 'the figure may fade' so that the word comes to signify 'carry away = mislead, deceive'. At all events, their method was not direct and open, but sly, secretive, cunning. They were sneaks. Using no doubt the back door rather than the front, these sellers of heresy would insinuate themselves in private. Choosing a time when the men were out (presumably at work), they concentrated their attention on *gullible women*. This expedient, comments Bishop Ellicott, was 'as old as the fall of man',[8] for the serpent first deceived Eve. It was also employed by the Gnostics, and has been the regular ploy of religious commercial travellers right up to and including the Jehovah's Witnesses of our own day.

The women chosen as victims Paul refers to by the word *gynaikaria*, 'little women', a term of contempt for women who were idle, silly and weak. Their weakness was double. First, they were morally weak, *loaded down with sins and . . . swayed by all kinds of evil desires*. Their sins were to them both a burden and a tyrant, and the false teachers, worming their way into their homes, played upon their feelings of guilt and of weakness. Second, they were intellectually weak, unstable, naive, gullible. They were the kind of women who were *always learning*, while at the same time they were *never able to come to a knowledge of the truth*. Quite incapable of reaching any settled convictions, they were like little boats tossed here and there by a storm (cf. Eph. 4:14). In such a state of mental confusion, people will listen to any teacher, however misleading. 'It was no love of truth that impelled them to learn,' however, 'but only a morbid love of novelty.'[9] Such women, weak in character and intellect, are an easy prey for door-to-door religious salesmen.

As an example of bogus teachers Paul now mentions *Jannes and Jambres*, the names (according to Jewish tradition) of the two chief magicians in Pharaoh's court. They are not named in the Old Testament

---

[8] Ellicott, p. 146.

[9] Ellicott, p. 146.

text, although one of the Targums inserts their names in Exodus 7:11 which reads: 'Pharaoh then summoned the wise men and sorcerers, and the Egyptian magicians also did the same things [miracles] by their secret arts.'

The implication of what Paul writes here is extremely important, although it does not lie on the surface. He draws a historical parallel between Jannes and Jambres who had opposed Moses centuries previously and *these teachers* (the false ones of his own day) who also oppose the truth. Jannes and Jambres were magicians; the false teachers also were 'evildoers' and 'impostors' (13). Perhaps they too went in for magic of some kind, for when the Ephesians who had 'practised sorcery' were converted, they had brought their books and publicly burned them (Acts 19:18–19). What is remarkable about this analogy, however, is not just that the Asian false teachers are likened to the Egyptian magicians, but also that Paul is likening himself to Moses! For Moses was the greatest figure of the Old Testament. No prophet arose like him in Israel, we are told, either in his knowledge of God ('whom the LORD knew face to face') or in the signs and wonders he did to authenticate the revelation of God (Deut. 34:10–11). 'See,' the Lord had said to him, 'I have made you like God to Pharaoh . . . You are to say everything I command you' (Exod. 7:1–2). So for forty years Moses spoke God's word and gave God's law to the people.

But now Paul dares to equate himself with Moses. For as Jannes and Jambres opposed Moses, so the Asian false teachers were opposing the truth. What truth? Why, the truth taught by Paul and entrusted by Paul to Timothy (1:14), the apostolic faith, the sacred deposit, which Timothy was to guard and to transmit. Thus the apostle Paul, naturally and without any apparent hesitation, puts himself on a level with Moses as one who also teaches God's truth. Moses taught the law; Paul preached the gospel. But whether it was law or gospel, the teaching of Moses the prophet or Paul the apostle, it was God's truth which people were opposing and rejecting.

So Paul rejects them as those who have *depraved minds*, despite their claim to *epignōsis* (knowledge), and are *rejected* (*adokimoi*, 'tried and found wanting') as to their *faith*. Moreover, he is confident that such people *will not get very far*. They may themselves 'go from bad to worse' (13). Their false teaching may also temporarily spread 'like gangrene' (2:17). But its success will be limited and transient. How could Paul be so sure? Because *their folly will be clear to everyone*, as it was (or 'came to be', *egeneto*, an aorist) *in the case of those men*, Jannes and Jambres.

We sometimes get distressed in our day – rightly and understandably – by the false teachers who oppose the truth and trouble the church, especially by the sly and slippery methods of backdoor religious traders. But we need have no fear, even if a few weak people may be taken in, even if falsehood becomes fashionable. For there is something blatantly false about heresy, and something self-evidently true about the truth. Error may spread and be popular for a time. But it *will not get very far*. In the end it is bound to be exposed, and the truth is sure to be upheld. This is a clear lesson of church history. Numerous heresies have arisen, and some have seemed likely to triumph. But today they are largely of historical interest. God has preserved his truth in the church.

Having reached the end of the first paragraph of chapter 3, it should now be plain to us what these dangerous seasons are which occur from time to time in 'the last days' in which we live, and how they arise. It is because in that part of God's field (the world) in which God has sown wheat, the devil has also sown weeds.[10] Changing the image, the devil has his 'fifth column', his secret agents, actually inside the church. As the Church of England's Article XXVI puts it: 'in the visible Church the evil [is] ever mingled with the good, and sometimes the evil have chief authority in the Ministration of the Word and Sacraments'. Yes, inside the church, within the visible society of professing believers, there are people of immoral character and conduct, of purely external religiosity, of corrupt mind and counterfeit faith. They are lovers of self, money and pleasure rather than lovers of God and other people. They retain the form of religion but deny its power. They oppose the truth and seek to win the weak to their harmful errors. Morally, religiously and intellectually they are perverse. It is a remarkably accurate portrayal of the so-called 'permissive society', which genially tolerates every conceivable deviation from Christian standards of righteousness and truth, and whose culture has crept into the church.

But Timothy is not to catch this infection, nor be carried away by this flood, but to stand out boldly against the prevailing fashion.

3. Standing firm in the faith (3:10–15a)

In this paragraph Paul twice addresses Timothy with the same two little Greek monosyllables *sy de*. They come at the beginning of verses 10

---

[10] Cf. Jesus' parable recorded in Matt. 13:24–30, 36–43.

and 14 (like the *sy oun* of 2:1) and are translated *You, however,* and *But as for you.* In stark contrast to the contemporary decline in morals, empty show of religion and spread of false teaching, Timothy is called to be different, and if necessary to stand alone.

Every Christian is called to be different from the world. 'Don't let the world around you squeeze you into its own mould' (Rom. 12:2, JBP). Certainly the pressures upon us to conform are colossal, not only from the direct challenge to traditional beliefs and morals, but also – and more – from the insidious, pervasive atmosphere of secularism which even seeps into the church. Many give in, often without realizing what they are doing. But again and again the Word of God addresses us, calling us not to be moved. We are not to be like a 'reed swayed by the wind', feebly bowing down before it from whatever direction it may blow. Rather, like a rock in a mountain torrent, we are to stand firm.

We might paraphrase the apostle's double appeal to Timothy in verses 10 to 14 like this: 'But as for you, in spite of all the current false teaching, what you have been closely following is *my* doctrine and *my* way of life, together with *my* purpose, faith, patience, love, endurance, persecutions and sufferings . . . Wicked people and impostors, deceiving others and themselves deceived, will still make their strange progress from bad to worse. But as for you, you are not to progress in any direction, least of all away from or beyond my teaching (for that would be to fall back, not to advance). On the contrary, you are to stand firm, to continue and keep to what you learned and have become convinced of, because you know those from whom you learned it.'

Paul first reminds Timothy what he has been doing so far: *you . . . know all about* or 'followed' *my teaching* (10). Then he encourages him to continue in the same path: *continue in what you have learned* (14). So verses 10 to 13 describe Timothy's *past* loyalty to the apostle, and verses 14 to 17 urge him to remain loyal in the *future.* The two main verbs sum up the gist of the paragraph: you have *followed* me faithfully up till now (10); so then *continue* to do so (14).

a. The past (3:10–13)

Timothy's position is explained in terms of a certain 'following' of Paul. The verb *parakoloutheō* can be used literally, of following a person as he or she goes somewhere and of walking in his or her footsteps. But it is not used in the New Testament like this. Its figurative use can refer either to an intellectual following, much as we say to a person who is explaining something to us 'I follow you', or to a real commitment of mind and life, as when we say of somebody 'he's a follower of so-and-so'. AG define these two meanings as to 'follow with the mind, understand, make one's own' and to 'follow faithfully, follow as a rule'. Luke uses the verb more or less in the former sense when he tells Theophilus of his meticulous historical research. He has 'carefully investigated everything from the beginning', he writes (Luke 1:3). But Paul seems to use the verb in the other and more committed sense in his letters to Timothy. In the first letter he has urged Timothy to nourish himself on 'the good teaching that you have followed', that is, embraced (1 Tim. 4:6). So surely the verb has the same meaning here in the second letter. Paul is reminding Timothy not simply that he has 'fully known' (AV) or 'observed' (RSV) his doctrine and conduct, as if he were merely an impartial student or a detached observer, but that he has become a dedicated disciple of the apostle's. No doubt he had begun by taking pains to grasp the meaning of Paul's instruction. But then he went further. He made it his own, believed it, absorbed it, lived by it. Similarly, he doubtless began by watching the apostle's way of life, but then he went on to imitate it. Because Paul knew himself as an apostle to be following Christ, he did not hesitate to invite others to follow himself: 'Follow my example,' he wrote, 'as I follow the example of Christ' (1 Cor. 11:1; cf. 1 Thess. 1:6). He even made himself the standard by which truth could be distinguished from error: 'Join together in following my example, brothers and sisters, and just as you have us as a model, keep your eyes on those who live as we do' (Phil. 3:17). So, in both belief and practice, in *teaching* and *way of life* (10), Timothy became and remained Paul's faithful follower. He had 'followed step by step' (NEB).

The contrast with the first paragraph of this chapter is obvious. The people described there were following their own inclinations (they were lovers of self, money and pleasure), and, sadly, their converts had been carried away by their own desires. Timothy, on the other hand, has followed an altogether different standard, namely the teaching and the example of Christ's apostle Paul. So Paul goes on to list the characteristics of his life, in contrast to that of the self-lovers whom he has characterized in verses 2–5. The emphatic words are the personal pronouns and possessive adjectives. They bring out the contrast clearly: 'For people will be lovers of themselves . . . *They* will be and do this and that. But as for *you*, Timothy, *you* (as distinct from *them*) have followed *me*, *my* teaching, *my* way of life, and so on.'

Why, however, does Paul give us this catalogue of his virtues and sufferings in verses 10 and 11? Is it not more than a little immodest, even conceited, that the apostle should put himself forward like this? Perhaps it is understandable that he should mention his *teaching*, but why go on to blow his own trumpet about his faith and love, his purpose and way of life, his sufferings and his endurance? Is it not rather inappropriate that he should boast like this?

No, Paul is not boasting. He has reasons quite other than a desire to show off for drawing attention to himself. He mentions his teaching first, and then goes on to supply two objective evidences of the genuineness of his teaching, namely the life he has lived and the sufferings he has endured. Indeed, these are good (though not infallible) general tests of people's sincerity, and even of the truth or error of their systems. Are they so convinced of their position that they both practise what they preach and are prepared to suffer for it? Have their beliefs made them better people, even in the face of opposition? Paul could answer both questions affirmatively. The false teachers lived lives of self-indulgence, and it would be quite out of character for them to be willing to suffer for their views; they were altogether too soft and easy-going for that. The apostle Paul, however, lived a consistent life of righteousness, self-control, faith and love, and remained steadfast to his principles through many severe persecutions.

Look at his behaviour first. Timothy had observed and tried to imitate Paul's *way of life* (*agōgē*, his whole demeanour), his *purpose* (the spiritual ambitions which motivated him and made life meaningful for him), his *faith* (which perhaps here includes his faithfulness), his *patience* (*makrothymia*, tolerance or long-suffering towards aggravating people), his *love* (towards both God and human beings, as opposed to the false teachers' love for self, money and pleasure) and his *endurance* (*hypomonē*, the patient putting up with trying circumstances, in distinction from *makrothymia*, the patient endurance of trying people). Indeed, since *hypomonē* is regularly in the New Testament the child of our Christian 'hope', our expectation of the Lord's return and the glory to follow, we may detect within this list yet another example of Paul's favourite triad of graces, 'faith, hope and love'.[11]

---

[11] See 1 Cor. 13:13; Col. 1:4–5; 1 Thess. 1:3; 2 Thess. 1:3–4; cf. Heb. 10:22–24.

The reference to *endurance* naturally leads on to the *persecutions* and the *sufferings* which Paul had had to endure. In particular, he mentions the three Galatian cities Antioch, Iconium and Lystra, because Timothy was a citizen of Lystra and had possibly himself witnessed the occasion when the apostle had been stoned by a hostile mob, dragged out of the city and left in the gutter for dead, though the Lord had rescued him from this and all other persecutions so far. Perhaps Paul's courage under persecution had even played a part in Timothy's conversion, much as Stephen's bravery in martyrdom had done in Paul's. At all events, Timothy knew about Paul's persecutions, first watching them, and then discovering that he must himself share in them, for he could not be committed to Paul's teaching and conduct without also becoming involved in his sufferings.[12]

In verse 12 Paul makes it clear that his experience was not unique. He sought to live *a godly life in Christ Jesus*, loving and serving God rather than himself, and he suffered for it. Timothy had found the same thing. For all Christian people who *in Christ Jesus* (i.e. through union with him) want to *live a godly life . . . will be persecuted*, and indeed are bound to suffer persecution. The godly arouse the hostility of the worldly. It has always been so. It was so for Christ, and he said it would be for us:

> If the world hates you, keep in mind that it hated me first. If you belonged to the world, it would love you as its own. As it is, you do not belong to the world, but I have chosen you out of the world. That is why the world hates you. Remember what I told you: 'A servant is not greater than his master.' If they persecuted me, they will persecute you also. (John 15:18–20; cf. 16:33)

It is important to notice the situation in which Christ here told his followers to expect persecution. He foresaw that they would be both in the world (living among godless people) and at the same time 'not belong to the world' (living a godly life in Christ). Those who are in Christ but not in the world are not persecuted, because they do not come into contact and therefore into conflict with their potential persecutors. Those who are in the world but not in Christ are also not persecuted, because the world sees nothing in them to persecute. The former escape persecution by withdrawal

---

[12] See Acts 13:14 – 14:23 for the Galatian cities Paul visited on his first missionary journey, and for the persecutions he endured there.

from the world, the latter by assimilation to it. It is only for those who are both in the world and in Christ at the same time that persecution becomes inevitable. As Calvin comments, 'it is in vain to try to detach Christ from his cross, and it is only natural that the world should hate Christ even in his members'.[13]

This inevitability of persecution is further explained in verse 13 by the continued activities of false teachers. Paul is quite outspoken about them. He dubs them *evildoers* and *impostors*. The latter word (*goēs*) means a 'sorcerer, juggler' and so in early Christian literature a 'swindler, cheat' (AG). The apostle does not credit them with sincerity; they are 'charlatans' (NEB). Such people *will go from bad to worse*. The verb for *go* (*prokoptō*) properly means to 'go forward, progress', but here Paul uses it ironically, since the only advance they make is backwards, not forwards, *from bad to worse*. He appears to be referring not to their success as teachers, for he has said that 'they will not get very far' (9), but to their own personal deterioration, both intellectual and moral. They are *deceiving and being deceived*. Alfred Plummer explains it well: 'they begin by being seducers and end in being dupes, and the dupes (very often) of their own deceptions; for deceit commonly leads to self-deceit'.[14]

b. The future (3:14–15)

So far in this paragraph Paul has been describing himself, but doing so in relation to Timothy, who has taken him as his guide. Timothy is seen to stand out in bold relief against the background of the prevalent evildoers and false teachers. For he has carefully followed Paul and modelled himself on Paul's teaching. Moreover, he has been right to do so, for Paul's teaching has been amply confirmed by his godly life and by his many persecutions endured bravely. Now for the second time Paul begins a sentence *But as for you* (*sy de*), distinguishing Timothy from the 'evildoers and impostors' he has just described. Previously he has contrasted their pursuit of their own inclinations with Timothy's faithful following of apostolic doctrine and example. Now he draws another contrast: they 'go' (though we have seen what a peculiar form their progress assumed), whereas Timothy is to *continue* in what he has learned and believed.

---

13 Calvin, p. 327.
14 Plummer, p. 385.

This kind of summons is frequently seen in the pages of the New Testament. It is especially relevant whenever innovators arise in the church, 'radicals' who claim to be progressive and who reject everything which smacks of the traditional. To be sure, the church of every generation must seek to translate the faith into contemporary ways of expressing it, to relate the unchanging Word to the changing world. But a translation is a rendering of the same message into another language; it is not a fresh composition. Yet this is what some modern theologians do, suggesting concepts of God and of Christ which Jesus and his apostles would not have recognized as their own. In such a situation we may perhaps be forgiven if, borrowing the Lord's own words, we say to them: 'no one after drinking old wine wants the new, for they say, "The old is better"' (Luke 5:39). The apostles themselves constantly warned their readers of newfangled ideas and called them back to the original apostolic message. Thus John declares that 'anyone who runs ahead and does not continue in the teaching of Christ does not have God', and encourages his flock, 'see that what you have heard from the beginning remains in you', for then they would 'remain in the Son and in the Father' (2 John 9; 1 John 2:24). Similarly here Paul tells Timothy to *continue* in what he has learned. In each of these verses the Greek verb is the same. Timothy had learned things and now firmly believed them. All right. Now he must *continue* in these things with endurance and not allow anyone to shift him from his ground.

The apostle now adds two reasons. His clear command to Timothy to continue, to cultivate stability in the truths he has learned, rests on two simple and plain arguments which he sets out in verses 14b and 15. Timothy must continue in *what* he has learned, because he knows from *whom* he has learned it. The teaching was guaranteed by the teacher. And who was this? The Greek manuscripts have two readings, one making *whom* plural and the other singular. The better attested is the plural (*para tinōn*), in which case the teachers referred to will include his grandmother Lois and his mother Eunice (who had indeed taught him from his infancy; see 1:5; 3:15) as well as the apostle Paul. Commentators who weigh the manuscript evidence go no further than to say that this reading is 'perhaps to be preferred'[15] or is 'probably correct'.[16] They agree that the alternative (the singular *para tinos*) is also well attested, however, and this would refer

---

[15] Ellicott, p. 152.
[16] Barrett, p. 113.

to the apostle Paul alone. Although the external authority for this reading is slightly less strong, the internal evidence seems to me to be more strongly in its favour. That is to say, in the immediate context Paul has been placing emphasis on the fact that Timothy has closely followed his teaching (10). That Paul's apostolic instruction was Timothy's model is stressed by the emphatic 'my' and 'me' of verses 10 and 11.

The wider context of the whole letter points the same way. In the first two chapters, the apostle has begged Timothy both to keep as the pattern of sound teaching 'what you heard from me' (1:13) and then to entrust to others 'the things you have heard me say' (2:2). It seems probable, therefore, that the phrase *you know . . . from whom you learned it* in 3:14 also refers to what Timothy has heard from Paul. Besides, the apostle is apparently giving *two* reasons for Timothy's continued loyalty; it is likely, therefore, that these will be distinct reasons and not both refer to his childhood education in the Scriptures.

In this case, the first ground of Timothy's confidence, and the first reason why he should continue in what he has learned, is that he has learned it from Paul. And he knows this Paul who has taught him. He has not only led him to Christ (1:2) and laid hands on him at his ordination (1:6), but he is also 'an apostle of Christ Jesus by the will of God' (1:1), to whom Christ had entrusted the deposit of the gospel (1:11–12), who has likened himself to Moses in his teaching of the truth (3:8), whose doctrine and example Timothy has loyally followed thus far, and who has confirmed his teaching by his consistent life and his bravery in persecution. Timothy was confident in Paul and his teaching authority, and we can share his confidence. Paul's gospel is still authenticated to us by his apostolic authority.

Timothy has not only learned Paul's gospel and known Paul's authority. *From infancy* he had been instructed in the Old Testament Scriptures, presumably by his mother and grandmother, and he was therefore extremely familiar with them. He believed them to be divinely inspired, as Paul is about to say. So the second reason why he must continue in what he has learned from Paul is its harmony with these very Scriptures. This was Paul's consistent claim. On trial before King Agrippa he had affirmed that he was teaching 'nothing beyond what the prophets and Moses said would happen – that the Messiah would suffer and, as the first to rise from the dead, would bring the message of light to his own people and to the Gentiles' (Acts 26:22–23). Similarly, at the beginning of his letter to the

Romans he had described God's gospel to which he was set apart as what God had 'promised beforehand through his prophets in the Holy Scriptures' (Rom. 1:2; cf. 3:21).

So, then, the reason why Timothy should remain loyal to what he has come firmly to believe is that he has learned it both from Old Testament Scripture and from the apostle Paul. The same two grounds apply today. The gospel we believe is the biblical gospel, the gospel of the Old Testament and of the New Testament, vouched for by both the prophets of God and the apostles of Christ. And we must resolve ourselves to pay attention to the encouragement which Paul addressed to Timothy and to continue in what we have learned because of this double authentication.

4. The origin and purpose of Scripture (3:15b–17)

Two central truths about Scripture are asserted here. The first concerns its origin (where it comes from) and the second its purpose (what it is intended for).

First, *All Scripture is God-breathed*. Some scholars, as in the NEB, have translated the opening words of verse 16: 'every inspired Scripture has its use'. Such a rendering would place a double limitation on Scripture. It would suggest that not all Scripture is inspired, and that therefore not all Scripture is useful, but only those parts which are inspired. Since the Greek sentence has no main verb, it is certainly legitimate, grammatically speaking, to supply the verb 'is' after, rather than before, the adjective 'God-breathed' and so translate 'every God-breathed Scripture is useful'. The argument against this construction, however, is that it does not do justice to the little word *and* (*kai*) which comes between the two adjectives *God-breathed* and *useful*. This 'and' suggests that Paul is asserting two truths about Scripture, namely that it is both God-breathed *and* useful, not merely one. For this reason we should render the sentence: 'all Scripture is God-breathed and useful'.

What does he mean by *all Scripture*? It seems to me not at all impossible that he is including by this comprehensive expression the two sources of Timothy's knowledge just mentioned, namely 'what you have learned' (from me) and 'the Holy Scriptures'. It is true that nowhere does the apostle explicitly call his epistles 'Scripture'. Nevertheless, on a number of occasions he gets very near it, and he certainly directs that his letters be read publicly in the Christian assemblies, no doubt alongside Old Testament readings (e.g. Col. 4:16; 1 Thess. 5:27). Several times he claims to be speaking in the name and with the authority of Christ (e.g. 2 Cor. 2:17; 13:3; Gal. 4:14), and calls his message 'the word of God' (e.g. 1 Thess. 2:13). Once he says that, in communicating to others what God has revealed to him, he speaks 'not in words taught us by human wisdom but in words taught by the Spirit' (1 Cor. 2:13). This is a claim to inspiration, indeed to verbal inspiration, which is the distinctive characteristic of 'Scripture'. Peter clearly regarded Paul's letters as Scripture, for in referring to them he calls the Old Testament 'the other Scriptures' (2 Pet. 3:16). In addition, it seems evident that Paul saw the possibility of a Christian supplement to the Old Testament because he could combine a quotation from Deuteronomy (25:4) with a saying of Jesus recorded by Luke (10:7) and call both 'Scripture' (1 Tim. 5:18).

His definition of Scripture, of *all Scripture*, is that it is *God-breathed*. The single Greek word *theopneustos* indicates not that Scripture itself or its human authors were breathed into by God, but that Scripture was breathed or breathed out by God. Scripture is not to be thought of as already in existence when (subsequently) God breathed into it, but as itself brought into existence by the breath or Spirit of God. There is no 'theory' or explanation of inspiration here, for no reference is made to the human authors, who (Peter says) 'spoke from God as they were carried along by the Holy Spirit' (2 Pet. 1:21). Nevertheless, it is clear from many passages that, however the process operated, it did not destroy the individuality or the active cooperation of the human writers. All that is stated here is that all Scripture is God-breathed. It originated in God's mind and was communicated from God's mouth by God's breath or Spirit. It is therefore rightly termed 'the Word of God', for God spoke it. Indeed, as the prophets used to say, 'the mouth of the Lord has spoken it'.

Second, Paul explains the purpose of Scripture: it is *useful*. And this is precisely because it is God-breathed. Only its divine origin secures and explains its usefulness to humankind. In order to show what this is, Paul uses two expressions. The first is in verse 15: *the Holy Scriptures*, he says, *are able to make you wise for salvation*. The Bible is essentially a handbook of salvation. Its overarching purpose is to teach not facts of science (e.g. the nature of moon rock) which we can discover by our own scientific investigation, but facts of salvation, which no space exploration can discover but only God can reveal. The whole Bible unfolds the divine scheme of salvation – the creation of men and women in God's image, our fall through disobedience into sin and under judgment, God's continuing love for us in spite of our rebellion, God's eternal plan to save us through his covenant of grace with a chosen people, culminating in Christ; the coming of Christ as the Saviour, who died to bear our sin, was raised from death, was exalted to heaven and sent the Holy Spirit; and our rescue first from guilt and alienation, then from bondage, and finally from mortality in our progressive experience of the freedom of God's children. None of this would be known apart from the biblical revelation. 'Scripture contains the perfect rule of a good and happy life.'[17]

More particularly, the Bible makes us wise for salvation *through faith in Christ Jesus*. So, since the Bible is a book of salvation, and since salvation is through Christ, the Bible focuses its attention upon Christ. The Old Testament foretells and foreshadows him in many and various ways; the Gospels tell the story of his birth and life, his words and works, his death and resurrection; the book of Acts describes what he continued to do and teach through his chosen apostles, especially in spreading the gospel and establishing the church from Jerusalem to Rome; the epistles display the full glory of his person and work, and apply it to the life of the Christian and the church; while Revelation shows Christ sharing the throne of God now and coming soon to complete his salvation and judgment. This comprehensive picture of Jesus Christ is intended to stimulate our *faith* in him, in order that by faith we may be saved.

Paul now goes on to show that the usefulness of Scripture relates to both belief and behaviour (16b–17). The false teachers divorced them; we must marry them. The NEB expresses the matter clearly. As for what we believe, Scripture is useful for teaching the truth and refuting error. As for how we behave, it is useful 'for reformation of manners and discipline in right living'. In each pair the negative and positive counterparts are combined. Do we hope, either in our own lives or in our teaching ministry, to overcome error and grow in truth, to overcome evil and grow in holiness? Then it is to Scripture that we must primarily turn, for Scripture is *useful* for these things.

Indeed, Scripture is the chief means which God employs to bring *the servant of God* to maturity. Who is intended by this expression is not explained. It may be a general term for every Christian, since the words

---

[17] Calvin, p. 330.

themselves mean no more than 'the person who belongs to God'. On the other hand, it was an Old Testament title of respect applied to some of God's spokesmen, such as Moses (Deut. 33:1), David (2 Chr. 8:14) and Elijah (1 Kgs 17:18), and Paul specifically addressed Timothy by this phrase in his first letter (6:11). It may, therefore, refer here to those called to positions of responsibility in the church, and especially to ministers whose task it is, under the authority of Scripture, to teach and refute, to reform and discipline. At all events, it is only by a careful study of Scripture that the servant of God may be *thoroughly equipped for every good work.*

Looking back over this chapter as a whole, we can appreciate the relevance of its message to our pluralist and tolerant society. The 'terrible times' in which we seem to be living are very distressing. We sometimes wonder if the world and the church have gone mad, so strange are their views, and so lax their standards. Some Christians are swept from their moorings by the flood of sin and error. Others go into hiding, as offering the best hope of survival, the only alternative to surrender. But neither of these is the Christian way. 'But as for you,' Paul says to us as he did to Timothy, 'stand firm. Never mind if the pressure to conform is very strong. Never mind if you are young, inexperienced, shy and weak. Never mind if you find yourself alone in your witness. You have followed my teaching so far. Now continue in what you have come to believe. You know the biblical credentials of your faith. Scripture is God-breathed and useful. Even in the midst of these grievous times in which evildoers and impostors go on from bad to worse, it can make you complete and it can equip you for your work. Let the Word of God make you an effective servant of God! Remain loyal to it, and it will lead you on into Christian maturity.'

2 Timothy 4:1–22

4. The charge to preach the gospel

This chapter contains some of the very last words spoken or written by the apostle Paul. They are certainly the last which have survived. He is writing within weeks, perhaps even within days, of his martyrdom. According to a fairly reliable tradition he was beheaded on the Ostian Way. For about thirty years without a break he has laboured as an apostle and a travelling evangelist. Truly, as he himself here writes, he has fought the good fight, finished the race and kept the faith (7). Now he awaits his reward, 'the crown of righteousness', which is in store for him in heaven (8). So these words are Paul's legacy to the church. They breathe an atmosphere of great solemnity. It is impossible to read them without being profoundly stirred.

The early part of the chapter takes the form of an impressive charge. *In the presence of God . . . I give you this charge*, he begins. The verb *diamartyromai* has legal connections and can mean to 'testify under oath' in a court of law or to require a witness to do so. It is used in the New Testament of any 'solemn and emphatic utterance' (MM). Paul's charge is addressed in the first instance to Timothy, his apostolic delegate and representative in Ephesus. But it is applicable in a secondary sense to everyone called to an evangelistic or pastoral ministry, even to all Christian people.

There are three aspects of the charge to be studied, namely its nature (precisely what Paul is commissioning Timothy to do), its basis (the arguments on which Paul grounds his charge) and a personal illustration of it from Paul's own example in Rome.

82

1. The nature of the charge (4:2)

Omitting verse 1 for the moment and passing to verse 2, the essence of the charge is in the three words *Preach the word*. We observe at once that the message Timothy is to communicate is called a *word*, a spoken utterance. Actually it is *the* word, God's word which God has spoken. Paul does not need to specify it further, for Timothy will know at once that it is the body of doctrine which he has heard from Paul and which Paul has now committed to him to pass on to others. It is identical with 'the deposit' of chapter 1. And in this fourth chapter it is equivalent to 'the sound doctrine' (3), 'the truth' (4) and 'the faith' (7). It consists of the Old Testament Scriptures, God-breathed and useful, which Timothy has known from infancy, together with the teaching of the apostle which Timothy 'knows all about', has 'learned' and has 'become convinced of' (3:10, 14). The same charge is laid upon the church of every age. We have no right to invent our message, but only to communicate *the word* which God has spoken and has now committed to the church as a sacred trust.

Timothy is to *preach* this word himself, to speak what God has spoken. His responsibility is not just to hear it, and to believe and obey what he hears; nor just to guard it from every falsification; nor just to suffer for it and continue in it; but now to preach it to others. It is good news of salvation for sinners. So he is to proclaim it like a herald in the marketplace (*kēryssō*; cf. *kēryx*, 'a herald', in 1:11). He is to lift up his voice without fear or favour, and boldly to make it known.

Paul goes on to list four marks which are to characterize Timothy's proclamation.

a. An urgent proclamation

The verb *ephistēmi*, *be prepared*, means literally to 'stand by', and so to 'be ready, be on hand' (AG). But here it appears to take on the flavour not just of alertness and eagerness, but of insistence and urgency. 'Never lose your sense of urgency' (JBP). Certainly it is no good preaching in an apathetic or careless manner. All true preaching conveys a sense of the urgent importance of what is being preached. Christian heralds know that they are handling matters of life and death. They are announcing the sinner's plight under the judgment of God, the saving action of God through the death and resurrection of Christ, and the summons to repent and believe.

How can they treat such themes with cold indifference? 'Whatever you do,' wrote Richard Baxter,

> let the people see that you are in good earnest . . . You cannot
> break men's hearts by jesting with them, or telling them a smooth
> tale, or patching up a gaudy oration. Men will not cast away their
> dearest pleasures upon a drowsy request of one that seemeth
> not to mean as he speaks, or to care much whether his request
> be granted.[1]

Such preaching, Paul adds, must continue *in season and out of season*. 'Press it home on all occasions, convenient or inconvenient' (NEB). This is not to be taken as an excuse for the insensitive rudeness which has sometimes characterized our evangelism and brought it into disrepute. We must not barge unceremoniously into other people's privacy or tread clumsily on their toes. No. The occasions Paul has in mind are probably 'welcome or unwelcome' (JB) not for the hearers so much as for the speaker. The translation of the NEB margin emphasizes this: 'be on duty at all times, convenient or inconvenient'. This takes the verb *ephistēmi* in its alternative sense, which is found sometimes in the papyri. It seems, then, that what we are given here is not a biblical warrant for rudeness, but a biblical appeal against laziness.

b. A relevant proclamation

The herald who announces the word is to *correct, rebuke and encourage*. This suggests three different ways of doing it. For God's Word is 'useful' for a variety of ministries, as Paul has already stated (3:16). It speaks to different people in different situations. Preachers must remember this and be skilful in their use of it. They must 'use argument, reproof, and appeal' (NEB), which is almost a classification of three approaches, intellectual, moral and emotional. For some people are tormented by doubts, and need to be convinced by arguments. Others have fallen into sin, and need to be rebuked. Others again are haunted by fears, and need to be encouraged. God's Word does all this and more. We are to apply it relevantly.

---

[1] *The Reformed Pastor* (1656; Epworth, 2nd edition revised, 1950), p. 145.

c. A patient proclamation

Although we are to be *prepared* (longing for people to make a ready response to the word), we are to be 'unfailing in patience' in waiting for it. We must never resort to the use of human pressure techniques, or attempt to contrive a 'decision'. Our responsibility is to be faithful in preaching the word; the results of the proclamation are the responsibility of the Holy Spirit, and we can afford to wait patiently for him to work. We are to be patient in our whole manner as well, for 'the Lord's servant . . . must be kind to everyone' and 'opponents must be gently instructed' (2:24–25). However solemn our commission and urgent our message, there can be no possible justification for a harsh or impatient manner.

d. An intelligent proclamation

We are not only to preach the word but to teach it, or rather to preach it with *careful instruction* (*kēryxon . . . en pasē . . . didachē*). C. H. Dodd made a distinction between *kērygma* and *didachē*, the former being the proclamation of Christ to unbelievers with a summons to repent, and the latter the ethical instruction of converts. The distinction is helpful and important. Yet, as has already been suggested in the comment on 1:11, it can be pressed too far. At the least, this verse shows that our *kērygma* must itself contain much *didachē*. Whether our proclamation is intended primarily to correct, rebuke or encourage, it must be a doctrinal ministry.

The Christian pastoral ministry is essentially a teaching ministry, which explains why candidates are required both to be orthodox in their own faith and to have an ability to teach (e.g. Titus 1:9; 1 Tim. 3:2). There is an increasing need, especially as the process of urbanization continues and standards of education rise, for Christian ministers to exercise in the teeming cities of the world a systematic expository preaching ministry, to *preach the word . . . with . . . careful instruction*. This is precisely what Paul had himself done in Ephesus, as Timothy well knew. For some three years he had continued to teach 'the whole will of God' both 'publicly and from house to house' (Acts 20:20, 27; cf. 19:8–10). Now Timothy must do the same.

This is Paul's charge to Timothy. He is to preach the word, and, as he announces the God-given message, to be ready to take up every opportunity, relevant in his application, patient in his manner and intelligent in his presentation.

2. The basis of the charge (4:1, 3–8)

It has already become apparent in the early chapters of this letter both that Timothy was a shy man and that the times in which he lived and worked were – to say the least – unpromising. He must have trembled as he read the apostle's solemn charge to him to keep preaching the word. He would have been tempted to shrink from such a responsibility. So Paul does more than issue a charge; he adds incentives. He bids Timothy look in three directions – first at Jesus Christ the coming Judge and King; second, at the contemporary scene; and third, at him, Paul, the aged prisoner approaching martyrdom.

a. The coming Christ (4:1)

Paul is not issuing his charge in his own name or on his own authority but *in the presence of God and of Christ Jesus* and therefore conscious of the divine direction and approval. Perhaps the strongest of all incentives to faithfulness is the sense of a commission from God. If Timothy can only be assured that he is the servant of the most high God and an ambassador of Jesus Christ, and that Paul's challenge to him is God's challenge, then nothing will deflect him from his task.

The main emphasis of this first verse, however, is not so much on the presence of God as on the coming of Christ. It is evident that Paul still believes in Christ's personal return. He wrote of it in his earliest letters, especially those to the Thessalonian church. Although he now knows that he will die before it takes place, yet still at the end of his ministry he looks forward to it, lives in the light of it and describes Christians as those who love Christ's appearing (8). He is sure that Christ will make a visible *appearing* (the word is *epiphaneia* in verses 1 and 8), and that when he appears he will both *judge the living and the dead* and consummate *his kingdom* or reign.

Now these three truths – the appearance, the judgment and the kingdom – should be as clear and certain an expectation to us as they were to Paul and Timothy. They cannot fail to exert a powerful influence on our ministry. For both those who preach the word and those who listen to it must give an account to Christ when he appears.

b. The contemporary scene (4:3–5)

Notice the word *for* or 'because' (*gar*) which introduces this paragraph. Paul is giving a second basis on which to ground his charge. It is another future event, not now the coming of Christ but, before that end point, the coming of dark and difficult days. Although the apostle seems to be anticipating that the situation will get worse, it is also plain from this paragraph and from what he has written earlier that such a time has already begun for Timothy. It is in the light of this contemporary scene that he issues further directions.

What are these times like? One characteristic is singled out, namely that people cannot bear the truth. Paul expresses it negatively and positively, and states it twice: They *will not put up with sound doctrine*, but will gather teachers *to suit their own desires* (3). They *will turn their ears away from the truth and turn aside to myths* (4). In other words, they cannot stand the truth and refuse to listen to it. Instead, they find teachers to suit the speculative ideas into which they are determined to wander. It all has to do with their ears, which (in the Greek sentence) are mentioned twice. They suffer from a peculiar pathological condition called *itching ears*, 'an itch for novelty'.[2] AG explain that the expression is a figure of speech for that kind of curiosity which 'looks for interesting and spicy bits of information'. Further, 'this itching is relieved by the messages of the new teachers'. In fact what the people do is stop their ears against the truth (cf. Acts 7:57) and open them to any teacher who will relieve their itch by scratching it.

Notice that what they reject is *sound doctrine* (3) or *the truth* (4), and what they prefer is *their own desires* (3) or *myths* (4). In this way they substitute their fancy for God's revelation. The yardstick by which they judge teachers is not (as it should be) God's Word but their own subjective taste. Worse still, they do not first listen and then decide whether what they have heard is true; they first decide what they want to hear and then select teachers who will oblige by toeing their line.

How is Timothy to react to this? We might guess that such a desperate situation should silence him. If people cannot bear the truth and will not listen to it, surely the sensible course will be for him to keep quiet? But Paul comes to the opposite conclusion. For the third time he uses those two little monosyllables *sy de*, *but you* (5; cf. 3:10, 14). He repeats his call to Timothy to be different. He must not take his lead from the fashions of the day.

Now follow four staccato commands which seem to be deliberately framed in relation to the situation in which Timothy finds himself and to the kinds of people to whom he is called to minister.

---

[2] Ellicott, p. 160.

1. Because the people are unstable in mind and conduct, Timothy is above everything else always to *keep your head*. Literally, *nēphō* means to 'be sober', and figuratively to 'be free from every form of mental and spiritual drunkenness' and so to 'be well-balanced, self-controlled' (AG). When men and women get intoxicated with heady heresies and sparkling novelties, ministers must keep 'calm and sane' (NEB).

2. Although the people will not listen to the sound teaching, Timothy must persist in teaching it and so be prepared to *endure hardship* because of the truth he refuses to compromise. Whenever the biblical faith becomes unpopular, ministers are sorely tempted to play down those elements which give most offence.

3. Because the people are woefully ignorant of the true gospel, Timothy is to *do the work of an evangelist*. It is not clear whether the reference is to a specialist ministry such as is implied in the only other New Testament passages where the word occurs (Acts 21:8; Eph. 4:11). The alternative is to interpret it as anybody who preaches the gospel and witnesses to Christ. In either case Paul is telling Timothy: 'make the preaching of the Good News your life's work' (JB). The good news is not just to be preserved against distortion; it is to be spread widely.

4. Even if the people forsake Timothy's ministry in favour of teachers who tickle their fancy, Timothy is to *discharge all the duties of his ministry*. The same verb is used when Paul and Barnabas had completed the relief work which they went to Jerusalem to do. They 'had finished their mission', Luke writes (Acts 12:25). In the same way Timothy must persevere until his task is accomplished.

Paul's four words of command, although different in detail, convey the same general message. Those difficult days, in which it was hard to gain a hearing for the gospel, were not to discourage Timothy; nor to deter him from his ministry; nor to induce him to trim his message to suit his hearers; still less to silence him altogether; but rather to spur him on to preach the more. It should be the same with us. The harder the times and the deafer the people, the clearer and more persuasive our proclamation must be. As Calvin puts it,

the more determined men become to despise the teaching of Christ, the more zealous should godly ministers be to assert it and the more strenuous their efforts to preserve it entire, and more than that, by their diligence to ward off Satan's attacks.[3]

c. The old apostle (4:6–8)

The third ground of the apostle's charge is yet another coming event, namely his own martyrdom. The link between this paragraph and verse 5 which comes before it is plain. Paul's argument runs like this: 'But as for *you*, Timothy, *you* must fulfil *your* ministry, for *I* am already on the point of death.' It is all the more vital for Timothy to continue and complete his ministry because the apostle's life work has reached completion and is about to close. As Joshua had followed Moses, and Solomon David, and Elisha Elijah, so now Timothy must follow Paul.

The apostle uses two vivid figures of speech to describe his coming death, one taken from the language of sacrifice and the other (probably) of boats. First, *I am already being poured out like a drink offering.* So imminent does he believe his martyrdom to be that he speaks of the sacrifice as having already begun. He goes on: *the time for my departure is near.* Departure (*analysis*) seems to have become a regular word for death, but we need not necessarily conclude from this that its metaphorical origin had been entirely forgotten. It means 'loosing' and could be used either of taking down a tent (which Lock favours,[4] because of the soldier's 'I have fought the good fight' in the following verse) or of 'release from shackles' (which Simpson mentions),[5] or of untying a boat from its moorings. The last is certainly the most vivid of the three possibilities. The two images then to some extent correspond,[6] for the end of this life (outpoured as a libation) is the beginning of another (putting out to sea). Already the anchor is weighed, the ropes are released, and the boat is about to set sail for another shore. Now, before the great adventure of his new voyage begins, he looks back over his ministry of about thirty years. He describes it – factually not boastfully – in three terse expressions.

First, *I have fought the good fight.* The words could equally well be translated 'I have run the great race' (NEB), for *agōn* denoted any contest involving physical effort, whether a race or a fight. But since the next

---

[3] Calvin, p. 334.

[4] Lock, p. 111.

[5] Simpson, p. 154.

[6] It is interesting that Paul used both metaphors during an earlier imprisonment, in which he had also faced the possibility of death (Phil. 2:17; 1:23).

phrase clearly refers to the race or course he has finished, it seems probable that Paul is again combining the soldier and athlete metaphors (as in 2:3–5), or at least the wrestling and running metaphors.

Next, he writes, *I have finished the race.* Some years previously, speaking to the elders of the very Ephesian church which Timothy was now leading, Paul had expressed his ambition to do just this. 'I consider my life worth nothing to me; my only aim is to finish the race and complete the task the Lord Jesus has given me' (Acts 20:24). Now he is able to say that he has done so. Both the verb and the noun he uses are the same. 'What had been a purpose was now a retrospect,' comments N. J. D. White.[7] He could use the perfect tense in each of these three expressions, as Jesus had done in the upper room,[8] because the end was so clearly in sight.

Third, *I have kept the faith.* This could perhaps mean 'I have kept faith with my Master'.[9] But in the context of this letter, which emphasizes so strongly the importance of guarding the deposit of revealed truth, it is more likely that Paul is affirming his faithfulness in this respect. 'I have safely preserved, as a guardian or steward, the gospel treasure committed to my trust.'

So the work of the apostle, and to a lesser extent of every gospel preacher and teacher, is pictured as fighting a fight, running a race, guarding a treasure. Each involves hard work, sacrifice and even danger. Paul has been faithful to the end in all three.

Now nothing remains for him but the prize, which he terms *the crown* [or better 'garland'] *of righteousness*, which is *in store* for him and which will be given him at the winning post *on that day.* Though intrinsically valueless, being made of evergreen leaves rather than of silver or gold, the garlands won by victors in the Greek games were greatly prized. 'Many a little town in those days', writes Bishop Handley Moule, 'took down a piece of its white wall in order that its son, crowned with the crown of the isthmus or of Olympia, might enter it *by a gate unused before.*'[10] The crown which Paul anticipates he calls *righteousness* (*dikaiosynē*). From his pen the word would most naturally mean 'justification'. But perhaps here it has a slightly different legal connotation, and is in deliberate contrast to the sentence he is expecting any day to receive from a human

---

[7] White, p. 178.

[8] John 17:4: 'having accomplished the work which thou gavest me to do' (RSV).

[9] Lock, p. 111.

[10] Moule, p. 145.

judge in a human court. The emperor Nero may declare him guilty and condemn him to death, but there will soon come a 'magnificent reversal of Nero's verdict'[11] when *the Lord, the righteous Judge*, declares him righteous.

The same vindication by Christ also awaits *all who have longed for his appearing*. This is not, of course, a doctrine of justification by good works. It is hardly necessary to emphasize Paul's continuing conviction that salvation is a free gift of God's grace, 'not because of anything we have done but because of his own purpose and grace' (1:9). The crown of righteousness is awarded to all those who 'have set their hearts on his coming appearance' (NEB), not because this is a commendable attitude to adopt but because it is a sure evidence of justification. Unbelievers, being unjustified, dread the coming of Christ (if they believe in it or think about it at all). Being unready for it, they will shrink in shame from Christ at his coming. Believers, on the other hand, having been justified, look forward to Christ's coming and have set their hearts upon it. Being ready for it, they will have boldness when Christ appears (1 John 2:28). Only those who have entered by faith into the benefit of Christ's first coming are eagerly awaiting his second (cf. Heb. 9:28).

This, then, is 'Paul the old man', as he described himself a year or two previously in his letter to Philemon (Phlm. 9). He has fought the good fight, finished the race and kept the faith. His lifeblood is on the point of being poured out. His little boat is about to set sail. He is eagerly awaiting his crown. These facts are to be Timothy's third spur to faithfulness.

Our God is the God of history. 'God is working his purpose out, as year succeeds to year.' 'He buries his workmen, but carries on his work.' The torch of the gospel is handed down by each generation to the next. As the leaders of the former generation die, it is all the more urgent for those of the next generation to step forward bravely to take their place. Timothy's heart must have been profoundly moved by this appeal from Paul the old warrior who had led him to Christ. Who led you to Christ? Is that person growing old? The man who introduced me to Christ is now living in retirement (though an active one!). We cannot rest for ever on the leadership of the preceding generation. The day comes when we must step into their shoes and ourselves take the lead. That day had come for Timothy. It comes to all of us in time.

---

[11] Simpson, p. 157.

So then, in view of the coming of Christ in judgment, of the contemporary world's distaste for the gospel and of the imprisoned apostle's imminent death, the latter's charge to Timothy had a note of solemn urgency: *preach the word!*

3. An illustration of the charge (4:9–22)

Paul does more than issue Timothy, from what might seem the safe distance of his prison cell, with an apostolic charge to preach the word; he gives him an illustration of it from his own example. For he himself has preached the word, not just throughout his ministry but very recently, boldly proclaiming the gospel in court when on trial for his life before imperial Rome.

Before we are ready to consider the details of this remarkable proclamation, however, we must understand the circumstances in which it took place.

From his majestic survey of the past ('I have fought the good fight . . .') and his confident anticipation of the future ('now there is in store for me the crown . . .') Paul returns in thought to the present and to his personal predicament. For the great apostle Paul is also a creature of flesh and blood, a man of similar nature and passions to us. Although he has finished his course and is awaiting his crown, he is still a frail human being with ordinary human needs. He describes his plight in prison, and expresses his loneliness in particular.

Several factors contributed to his sense of isolation, and he describes these openly. He had been deserted by his friends (9–13); he had been opposed by Alexander the metalworker (14–15); and he had been unsupported at his first defence (16–18).

a. Deserted by his friends (4:9–13 and 19–21)

It is quite true that Paul has not been left entirely friendless. This becomes clear if at this point we glance on to the end of the chapter. Paul mentions here, first, his friends overseas (19), and he sends them a message of greeting. Prisca and Aquila, whom he has called his 'fellow workers in Christ Jesus' (Rom. 16:3) and with whom he stayed in Corinth (Acts 18:2; 1 Cor. 16:19), are clearly still in Ephesus where we last heard of them in the Acts record (18:26). So is *the household of Onesiphorus*, although, as was suggested in the comment on 1:16–18, it seems that Onesiphorus himself is still separated from his family and in Rome.

Paul next sends Timothy items of news about two other mutual friends (20). Erastus, he says, *stayed in Corinth*. It may well be right to identify him with the Erastus who is described as Corinth's 'director of public works' (Rom. 16:23) and with the Erastus whom Paul sent with Timothy into Macedonia (Acts 19:22). The fact that Paul needs to inform Timothy that Erastus stayed in Corinth suggests that after Paul's re-arrest he may have accompanied the prisoner as far as Corinth on his way to Rome. The other news item concerns Trophimus, who was a native of Ephesus and had been one of Paul's companions during his third missionary journey at least in Greece and Troas and on the voyage to Jerusalem (Acts 20:1–5; 21:29). We do not know the circumstances in which Paul left him ill at Miletus, the port near Ephesus.

In these final verses of the letter the apostle also mentions some Christians in Rome, who send their greetings to Timothy. He gives the names of three men – Eubulus, Pudens and Linus (the last just possibly the Linus whom Irenaeus and Eusebius mention as the first bishop of Rome following the martyrdom of Peter and Paul) – and of one woman, Claudia, and then mentions *all the brothers and sisters*. It seems likely, since Paul knows some of their names and can send greetings from them to Timothy, that they have visited him in prison.

Nevertheless, the apostle feels himself terribly cut off and abandoned, exiled from the churches he founded and from the people in them he knows and loves. More distressing still is the fact that a number of his close circle of travelling companions have – for a variety of reasons – left him or become separated from him. It is their fellowship that he misses more than anybody's. In verses 10 and 12 he mentions four in particular: Demas, Crescens, Titus and Tychicus.

The desertion of Demas is obviously extremely painful to Paul. He was previously one of his close associates or 'fellow workers'. In the two other New Testament verses in which he is mentioned his name is coupled with Luke's (Col. 4:14; Phlm. 24). But now, instead of setting his love on Christ's future appearing (8), *he loved this world* (literally, 'age'). We are not told the details. Bishop Moule may have been right to guess that he was 'smitten with cowardice in that reign of terror'.[12] The other three are not criticized for their departure. Crescens, whose name does not appear elsewhere in the New Testament, has *gone to Galatia* (perhaps here

---

[12] Moule, p. 150.

meaning Gaul), and Titus, who must by now have finished his task in Crete, has travelled to Dalmatia on the Eastern Adriatic coast. No reason is given for these movements. Of Tychicus, however, Paul says: *I sent him to Ephesus* (12). Twice described as 'the dear brother and faithful servant in the Lord', he has been sent on several responsible missions before, apparently carrying Paul's letters to the Ephesians, to the Colossians and to Titus (Eph. 6:21–22; Col. 4:7–8; Titus 3:12). It looks as if he is now being entrusted with the last of all Paul's letters, this one to Timothy. It may be that Paul also intends him to replace Timothy in Ephesus while the latter is absent visiting Paul in Rome.

Here, then, are four close and trusted fellow labourers whom Paul sorely misses, although (except Demas) their absence is on the Lord's business. He goes on: *Only Luke is with me* (11). It is a touching testimony to the unwavering loyalty of the apostle's companion and 'our dear friend Luke, the doctor' (Col. 4:14). Apart from this solitary exception of Luke, however, Paul is alone in prison for various reasons, good and bad. He feels it keenly. He longs and asks for three things: first, for people to keep him company; second, for a cloak to keep him warm; third, for scrolls and parchments to keep him occupied.

First, companions. He asks Timothy: *Get Mark and bring him with you* (11). Mark had been a deserter on the first missionary journey (Acts 12:25; 13:13; 15:38–39). Later, however, he was restored (Col. 4:10; Phlm. 24; 1 Pet. 5:13), and now *he is helpful to* Paul.

But above all Paul yearns for Timothy himself. *Do your best to come to me quickly*, he writes (9). *Do your best to get here before winter* (21). If he is ever to see Timothy again and enjoy his friendship, then Timothy must come quickly (while he is still alive) and in any case before winter (when navigation would be impossible). So he twice urges him to do his best to come. We must not play down the urgency of Paul's affectionate desire to see Timothy. The same apostle who has set his love and hope upon the coming of Christ (8) nevertheless also longs for the coming of Timothy. 'I long to see you,' he has written at the beginning of his letter, 'so that I may be filled with joy' (1:4). The two longings are not incompatible. We sometimes meet super-spiritual people who claim that they never feel lonely and have no need of human friends, for the companionship of Christ satisfies all their needs. But human friendship is the loving provision of God for humanity. It was God himself who said in the beginning: 'It is not good for the man to be alone' (Gen. 2:18). Wonderful as are both the presence of the Lord Jesus every day and the prospect of his coming on the last day, they are not intended to be a substitute for human friendships.

Warm clothing is necessary to Paul as well as companionship. So he urges Timothy: *When you come, bring the cloak that I left with Carpus at Troas* (13). It seems probable that the *phailonēs* (*cloak*) was the equivalent of the Latin *paenula*, 'an outer garment of heavy material, circular in shape with a hole in the middle for the head'.[13] It was no doubt in anticipation of the coming winter (21) that Paul felt the need of the extra warmth it could give him. But as for who Carpus was, and why Paul left his belongings with him in Troas, we can only guess. Bishop Moule suggests that it was in the house of Carpus at Troas both that the 'memorable Eucharist' was held (Acts 20:1ff.) and that years later Paul was arrested and carried off, with no opportunity to gather his possessions together.[14]

The third necessity Paul mentions is *my scrolls, especially the parchments* (13). The difference between the two is probably that the former were made of papyrus rather than parchment. These papyrus rolls may have been writing materials or his correspondence, or some official documents, even perhaps his certificate of Roman citizenship. The parchments may conceivably have been unused (NEB, 'my notebooks'). But it seems more probable that they were 'books' of some kind, and the most likely guess is 'Paul's version of the Old Testament in Greek, no small burden to carry around',[15] and/or 'possibly official copies of the Lord's words or early narratives of his life'.[16]

These, then, were Paul's three conscious needs. Later he says that during his first defence in court 'the Lord stood at my side and gave me strength' (17), and no doubt he enjoyed the companionship and strength of the Lord Jesus in his dungeon as well. Yet the help he obtained from his Lord was indirect as well as direct. He did not despise the use of means. Nor should we. When our spirit is lonely, we need friends. When our body is cold, we need clothing. When our mind is bored, we need books. To admit this is not unspiritual; it is human. These are the natural needs of mortal men and women. As Bishop Moule wisely says, we are

---

[13] Guthrie, p. 173.

[14] Moule, pp. 157f.

[15] Hanson, p. 102.

[16] Lock, p. 118.

'never for one moment denaturalized by grace'.[17] We must not, then, deny our humanity or frailty, or pretend that we are made of other stuff than dust.

Of course, some Christians today scorn reading and study altogether, and assert that they would not feel the need of books at any time, let alone in prison. Let Calvin answer them:

> Still more does this passage refute the madness of the fanatics
> who despise books and condemn all reading and boast only of their
> *enthusiasmous*, their private inspirations by God. But we should note
> that this passage commends continual reading to all godly men as a
> thing from which they can profit.[18]

Several commentators point out the historical parallel between Paul's imprisonment in Rome and William Tyndale's in Belgium nearly fifteen centuries later. Here is Handley Moule's description of Tyndale and quotation from his letter:

> In 1535, immured by the persecutor at Vilvorde in Belgium, he wrote,
> not long before his fiery martyrdom, a Latin letter to the Marquis
> of Bergen, Governor of the Castle: 'I entreat your lordship, and that
> by the Lord Jesus, that if I must remain here for the winter you would
> beg the Commissary to be so kind as to send me, from the things of
> mine which he has, a warmer cap; I feel the cold painfully in my
> head. Also a warmer cloak, for the cloak I have is very thin. He has
> a woollen shirt of mine, if he will send it. But most of all, my Hebrew
> Bible, Grammar and Vocabulary, that I may spend my time in that
> pursuit.'[19]

b. Opposed by Alexander the metalworker (4:14–15)

The second contributing factor to Paul's ordeal was the fierce opposition he had sustained to himself and his message from a man named *Alexander*. We know that his trade was that of a *metalworker*, or worker in bronze, for this is how Paul describes him. But we do not know his identity.

---

[17] Moule, p. 152.

[18] Calvin, p. 341.

[19] Moule, pp. 158f.

It is unlikely that Alexander the metalworker was the same person as Alexander the heretic (1 Tim. 1:20) or Alexander the orator (Acts 19:33), for the name was a common one. Nor do we know what the *great deal of harm* was which he had done to the apostle. A. T. Hanson points out that, literally translated, Alexander 'informed many evil things against me' and that 'the regular word for an informer is connected with this verb'.[20] So some commentators suggest that Alexander was the informer responsible for Paul's second arrest. If this happened at Troas, it might explain why Timothy, who will pass through Troas on his journey to Rome (13), is warned: *you too should be on your guard against him.* But Alexander did more than inform: *he strongly opposed our message.* We may be quite sure that it was Paul's concern for the truth of the message, and not personal pique or vindictiveness, which led him to express his belief (it is a statement, according to the best manuscripts, not a wish or a prayer): *The Lord will repay him for what he has done.*

c. Unsupported at his first defence (4:16–18)

Some have thought that Paul's *first defence* is a reference to his first imprisonment and that the proclamation of the word to the Gentiles (which he mentions in the following verse) was due to his release from this imprisonment.[21] The context seems, however, to require a reference to some more recent event. So most commentators understand his *first defence* to have been the first hearing of his case, 'the preliminary investigation preceding the formal trial'.[22]

Now Roman law would have permitted him to employ an advocate and call witnesses. But, as Alfred Plummer puts it,

> among all the Christians in Rome there was not one who would stand at his side in court either to speak on his behalf, or to advise him in the conduct of his case, or to support him by a demonstration of sympathy.[23]

At my first defence, no one came to my support, but everyone deserted me. Yet if ever an accused man needed help, it was now. We are not told what charges had been laid against him. But we know from Tacitus, Pliny and

---

[20] Hanson, p. 102.
[21] So Eusebius, 11.22.1–8.
[22] Guthrie, p. 175.
[23] Plummer, p. 420.

other contemporary writers the kinds of allegations which were being made against Christians at that time. They were supposed to be guilty of horrid crimes against the state and against civilized society. They were accused of 'atheism' (because they shunned idolatry and emperor-worship), of cannibalism (because they spoke of eating Christ's body), and even of a general 'hatred of the human race' (because of their supposed disloyalty to Caesar and perhaps because they had renounced the popular pleasures of sin). It may be that some of these charges were being levelled against Paul. Whatever the case for the prosecution, he had no-one to defend him but himself. Either because Christian friends could not or would not, he was unsupported and alone.

This moment, one might cautiously say, was Paul's Gethsemane. Of course his agony was different from Christ's. Yet like his Master before him he had to face his ordeal alone, for at the time of his greatest need he could say *everyone deserted me*, as it is written of Christ 'everyone deserted him and fled' (Mark 14:50). Lock goes even further and, noting nine verbal similarities between Psalm 22 and verses 10 and 16–18 of this chapter, asks: 'had St. Paul, like his Master, been saying this Psalm in the hour of his desertion?'[24] Certainly, again like his Master, he prayed that their sin might *not be held against them*. There is no need, incidentally, to make out that there is an irreconcilable discrepancy between this prayer and the statement about Alexander two verses previously. The cases were quite different. For Alexander had actually spoken against the gospel from deliberate malice, whereas Paul's friends in Rome had failed to speak at all, and their silence was due not to malice but to fear.

Nevertheless, once more like his Master, Paul knew that he was *not* alone. In anticipation of the coming desertion, Jesus said, 'A time is coming and in fact has come when you will be scattered, each to your own home. You will leave me all alone. Yet I am not alone, for my Father is with me' (John 16:32). Similarly Paul could say that, although *everyone deserted me* (16), yet *the Lord stood at my side and gave me strength* (17). Christ's presence at Paul's side and his gift to him of inward strength (the verb is *endynamoō* as in 2:1 and Phil. 4:13) both strengthened him to preach the gospel to all the Gentiles present and led to his rescue (at least temporarily) *from the lion's mouth.*

---

[24] Lock, p. 116.

There is much speculation about the identity of the *lion*. We can be certain that there is no reference to the lions of the amphitheatre, for there was never any question that this might be his fate as a Roman citizen. The early Greek commentators believed that Paul was referring obliquely to Nero, 'on account of his cruel nature',[25] and A. T. Hanson points out that, according to Josephus, the news of the emperor Tiberius's death in AD 37 'reached Herod Agrippa in the cryptic form "the lion is dead"'.[26] Other guesses are that the lion is Satan (as in 1 Pet. 5:8), or Paul's human prosecutor in court, or death, or, more generally still, the great danger in which his enemies had placed him (as in Pss 22:21; 35:17). At all events Paul emerges from this incident as a New Testament Daniel for whose protection the Lord shut the lion's mouth. In the future too, Paul goes on confidently, *the Lord will rescue me*, not indeed from death (for he is expecting to die, 6), but *from every evil attack* outside God's permitted will. He will also *bring me safely to his heavenly kingdom*, though Nero may soon dispatch me from my earthly kingdom.

We are now in a position to see what a superb illustration the apostle is giving Timothy of his charge to 'preach the word'. Paul is on trial for his life. He has been deserted by his friends (who have left him in the lurch or been unable to help him), opposed by his enemies and unsupported in his trial by any barrister or witness. So he is alone. Surely now he will think of himself for a change? Surely now he will demonstrate at least a little self-pity? Surely now he will defend himself and plead his cause? Perhaps he did answer the charges laid against him, for he refers to the trial as his *defence* (16). Yet even now, although in grave personal danger, facing the probability of a death sentence, his dominant concern is not himself but Christ; not to be a witness in his own defence but a witness to Christ; not to plead his own cause but the cause of Jesus Christ.

In one of the highest tribunals of the empire, before his judges and perhaps before the emperor himself, no doubt with a large crowd of the general public present, Paul 'preached the word'. Or, as he himself expresses it: *the Lord stood at my side and gave me strength, so that through me the message might be fully proclaimed and all the Gentiles might hear it*. If ever there has been a sermon preached 'out of season', this was it!

[25] Eusebius, 11.22.4.
[26] Hanson, p. 103.

All he tells us about its content is that he fully proclaimed the *kērygma*. That is, he took the opportunity to expound the gospel in its fullness, the good news of Jesus Christ incarnate, crucified, risen, reigning and coming again. Only because of this could he claim as he has done, 'I have finished the race' (7).

Alfred Plummer gives a graphic description of the scene as he envisages it:

> It is quite possible that this event, which the Apostle of the Gentiles regards as the completing act of his own mission and ministry, took place in the forum itself . . . But at any rate it would be held in a court to which the public had access; and the Roman public at this time was the most representative in the world . . . In that representative city and before that representative audience he preached Christ; and through those who were present and heard him the fact would be made known throughout the civilized world that in the imperial city and before the imperial bench the Apostle of Christ had proclaimed the coming of his kingdom.[27]

This, then, is to be Timothy's model. He has in past days followed Paul in his doctrine, behaviour and sufferings (3:10–11); he could safely follow Paul's example in this also. For in issuing the solemn charge to Timothy to preach the word, and do it urgently, Paul has not sidestepped the challenge himself. On the contrary, he has enforced his charge, not only from Christ's coming, the contemporary scene and his impending death, but also by the shining example he has himself just set in the imperial court at a moment of great personal loneliness and peril.

d. Conclusion

Underlying this whole letter is Paul's basic conviction that God has spoken through his prophets and apostles, and that this unique revelation – 'the faith', 'the truth', 'the word', 'the gospel', the 'sound teaching' – has been committed to the church as a sacred treasure or 'deposit'.

Now the apostle, who throughout his three decades of active ministry has faithfully delivered to others what he himself had received, is on his deathbed. He is on the very point of being sacrificed. He seems to have

---

27 Plummer, pp. 425f.

caught a glimpse with his mind's eye of the gleaming steel of the executioner's sword. So he burns with a passionate longing that Timothy, his young but trusted lieutenant, will step into his shoes, carry on from where he has had to stop, and pass on the torch to others.

Paul is fully alert to the difficulties, however, both internal and external. Timothy himself is inexperienced, infirm and shy. The world's opposition is strong and subtle. And behind these things stands the devil, bent on 'taking people alive' and keeping them prisoner. For the devil hates the gospel and uses all his strength and cunning to obstruct its progress, now by perverting it in the mouths of those who preach it, now by frightening them into silence through persecution or ridicule, now by persuading them to advance beyond it into some fancy novelty, now by making them so busy with defending the gospel that they have no time to proclaim it.

So then, knowing the sacred deposit entrusted to him, the nearness of his own martyrdom, the natural weaknesses of Timothy, the opposition of the world and the extreme subtlety of Satan, Paul issues to Timothy his fourfold charge regarding the gospel: to guard it (because it is a priceless treasure), to suffer for it (because it is a stumbling block to the proud), to continue in it (because it is the truth of God) and to proclaim it (because it is good news of salvation).

Timothy was called to be faithful in his generation; where are the men and women who will be faithful in ours? They are urgently needed. No doubt our response will be: 'Who is equal to such a task?' If so, we need to consider two brief expressions in the final verses of the letter, which I have so far passed by.

First, in verse 22: *The Lord be with your spirit. Grace be with you all.* These are the very last recorded words of the apostle. If he has been dictating thus far (perhaps to Luke), it is possible that he now takes the pen himself and writes this as his autograph. May *the Lord be with you* (singular), he prays, as he has been with me during my trial (17). And may *grace* [the word in which all Paul's theology is distilled] *be with you*. This time the pronoun *you* is plural (NIV *with you all*), which 'recognizes that the letter was in fact destined for public use'.[28] It was directed to the whole church. It is directed to us today.

Then in verse 18 we read, *To him be glory for ever and ever. Amen.* It would be difficult to find a better summary than these two sentences of

---

28 Barrett, p. 125.

the apostle's life and ambition. First, he received grace from Christ. Then he returned glory to Christ. 'From him grace; to him glory.' In all our Christian life and service we should embrace no other way of thinking than this.

Study guide

The aim of this study guide is to help you get to the heart of what John Stott has written, and to challenge you to apply what you learn to your own life. The questions have been designed for use by individuals or by small groups of Christians meeting, perhaps for an hour or two each week, to study, discuss and pray together.

The guide provides material for each of the sections in the book. When used by a group with limited time, the leader should decide beforehand which questions are most appropriate for the group to discuss during the meeting and which should perhaps be left for group members to work through by themselves or in smaller groups during the week.

In order to be able to contribute fully and to learn from the group meetings, each member of the group needs to read through the section or sections under discussion, together with the passages in the letter to which they refer.

It is important not to let these studies become merely academic exercises. Guard against this by making time to think through and discuss how what you discover *works out in practice* for you. Make sure you begin and end each study by focusing on God in praise and prayer. Ask the Holy Spirit to speak to you through your discussion together.

ⓠ Introduction (pp. 1–9)

1 On what grounds is it suggested that this letter may not in fact have been written by the apostle Paul (pp. 2ff.)?

2 How may these objections be answered? Who do you think wrote 2 Timothy?

3 How do we know that this letter was written from a prison cell (p. 4)? What implications does this have for the way we read it?

4 In what ways was Timothy 'hopelessly unfit' (p. 7) to assume a significant role of leadership in the church? Does this have anything to say to you?

5 'The church of our day urgently needs to take to heart the message of this second letter of Paul to Timothy' (p. 9). Do you agree? Why?

ⓠ 2 Timothy 1:1–18
1. The charge to guard the gospel (pp. 11–32)

1. Paul, an apostle of Christ Jesus (1:1)

1 In what way is Paul making 'a considerable claim for himself' (p. 11) in verse 1? How can he justify this?

2 What do you think Paul means by 'the life that is in Christ Jesus' (verse 1)? Have you begun to experience this? If so, can you put into words exactly how it happened?

2. Timothy, Paul's dear son (1:2–8)

1 In what way is Timothy a 'son' of Paul? Do you have any 'children' in this sense? Who are you able to identify as your 'parents'?

2 What does it really mean to wish someone 'grace, mercy and peace' (verse 2)?

3 What are the 'four major influences' (pp. 14ff.) which had shaped Timothy's life? Are you aware of similar factors at work in your own life?

....

'Anyone who has been born and bred in a Christian home has received from God a blessing beyond price.' (p. 15)

....

4 What is the gift of God which Timothy received when Paul laid hands on him likely to have been (p. 16)? How do we know?

5 What spiritual gifts have you received? How do you know? In what ways might what Paul says to Timothy apply to you?

6 What two truths are 'impossible to systematize into a tidy doctrine' (p. 18)? How are these reflected in the experience of Paul and Timothy? And in your experience too?

7 What are the 'three main ways' (p. 20) in which Christians are tempted to feel ashamed? How about you?

3. God's gospel (1:9–10)

1 In what ways is salvation 'far more than forgiveness' (p. 21)? Why is this so important for the way the gospel is proclaimed today?

2 How does Paul underline the truth that our salvation cannot come from ourselves and what we do?

3 What is the 'doctrine of election' (p. 22)? How does it bring about 'deep humility and gratitude' as well as 'peace and assurance'?

4 It is clear that people still die. So how can Paul claim that Jesus has 'destroyed death' (p. 23)? What does he mean?

5 'One of the most searching tests to apply to any religion concerns its attitude to death' (p. 25). Discuss your own experience of Christianity in relation to this statement.

6 What are the five stages that the author identifies 'by which God's saving purpose unfolds' (p. 26)?

4. Our duty in relation to God's gospel (1:11–18)

1 What do the terms 'apostle', 'herald' and 'teacher' mean in relation to the gospel (pp. 26f.)?

2 What is the particular significance of the term 'testimony' in verse 8 (p. 27)? How does this apply to you?

3 Why does sharing the gospel involve suffering? In what ways have you found this to be true in your experience?

....

'No-one can preach Christ crucified with faithfulness and escape opposition, even persecution.' (p. 28)

....

4 In what senses is Paul's teaching to be a pattern for Timothy (pp. 28f.)?

5 Why does the gospel need to be guarded so carefully? In what ways does the truth of the gospel come under attack in your situation? How can you 'guard' it?

6 What reassurance is there for those who doubt their ability to carry out their responsibilities in relation to the gospel (pp. 31f.)?

ⓠ 2 Timothy 2:1–26
2. The charge to suffer for the gospel (pp. 33–60)

1. Handing on the truth (2:1–2)
1 When Paul tells Timothy to 'be strong in the grace that is in Christ Jesus' (verse 1), what exactly does he mean? Be as practical as you can.
2 What four stages in 'the handing down of the truth' (pp. 34f.) can be identified here? How do we today fit into this sequence?

2. Metaphor I: the dedicated soldier (2:3–4)
1 What parallels between the soldier and the Christian does Paul highlight?
2 Can you think of things which, although 'perfectly innocent in themselves' (p. 37), actually hinder you as a soldier of Christ? What are you going to do about this?

3. Metaphor II: the law-abiding athlete (2:5)
1 In what ways is the Christian life like a race?
2 What 'rules' (p. 38) are there that we need to keep in order to win through?

4. Metaphor III: the hardworking farmer (2:6)
1 What sorts of 'harvest' (pp. 39f.) is Paul referring to here?
2 In what ways do you find the Christian life to be 'hard work'? Should it be like this, do you think? Why?

5. The way to understanding (2:7)
1 What 'important biblical balance' (p. 41) is set out here?
2 In what way is this verse 'a good example of Paul's self-conscious apostolic authority' (p. 42)?
3 Which do you tend to concentrate on in Bible study: 'thought' or 'prayer'? What do you think Paul might say to you?

6. Suffering a condition of blessing (2:8–13)
1 How is what Paul says here about Jesus a 'full . . . account of the gospel' (p. 43)?
2 How does remembering what happened to Jesus help the Christian who is facing suffering?

3 In what sense did Paul's sufferings help to secure the salvation of others? Have you experienced anything like this?

4 What does Paul mean by 'died with him' in verse 11b? How does this apply to you?

5 What does 'he remains faithful' mean in verse 13 (p. 46)?

6 How would you answer someone who objected to the suggestion that there is something that God 'cannot' do (pp. 46f.)?

7 What is the 'single lesson' (p. 47) that Paul has been hammering home in verses 1–13? In what ways have you found this to be true?

7. Metaphor IV: the unashamed worker (2:14–19)

1 In the area of Christian ministry, how can you tell the difference between a 'good' and a 'bad' worker (pp. 48f.)?

2 What is the 'word of truth' (p. 49)? What does it take to communicate it effectively?

3 What specific damage is caused by false teaching? What is 'most revealing' about these 'two tendencies of heresy' (p. 51)? In what ways are you aware of these things today?

4 How does verse 19 help to fill out what Paul is saying here?

8. Metaphor V: the clean article (2:20–22)

1 To what do the two different sorts of articles in these verses refer?

....

'No higher honour could be imagined than to be an instrument in the hand of Jesus Christ.' (p. 53)

....

2 What is the 'essential condition' (p. 53) which makes teachers useful to Jesus? Can you think of ways in which you could fulfil this condition more fully?

3 What does Paul tell Timothy to avoid? Why does he use a term as strong as 'flee' (p. 54)?

4 What does Paul tell Timothy to aim for? Why does he use a term as strong as 'pursue' (p. 55)?

5 Can you think of anything you should be avoiding which you are actually pursuing? Or anything you should be pursuing which you are in fact avoiding?

9. Metaphor VI: the Lord's servant (2:23–26)

1 How would you answer someone who suggested that Paul is outlawing all forms of controversy in these verses? What does he mean, then?

2 What experience have you had of 'the combination of unbiblical speculations and uncharitable attacks' (p. 57)? Why does this do so much damage?

3 What characteristics of Christian leadership does Paul highlight here? Why are these so important?

4 What 'link . . . between the moral and the intellectual' (p. 59) is illustrated here? Can you think of examples of this from your own experience?

5 How is the devil's activity characterized here? What does this perspective tell you about the work of the Christian teacher?

2 Timothy 3:1–17
3. The charge to continue in the gospel (pp. 61–81)

1. Facing terrible times (3:1–2a)

1 What does Paul want to make sure that Timothy understands? Why does he lay such stress on this?

2 What are 'the last days' (p. 62)? What is it about them that Timothy needs to know? How is this relevant to us today?

2. The evil people are described (3:2–9)

1 What is the fundamental characteristic of the people Paul describes here?

2 What do the features Paul sets out have in common?

3 How is it possible to be religious and yet still demonstrate the characteristics listed in verses 2–4?

4 Is yours a 'true religion' (p. 67)? How do you know?

5 What is 'indeed astonishing' (p. 68) about the sorts of people Paul is describing?

6 What marks out the efforts of the false teacher?

7 What is so 'remarkable' (p. 69) about Paul's discussion of Jannes and Jambres?

8 Can you think of any 'fashionable' falsehoods (p. 70) which have since faded away?

....

'There is something blatantly false about heresy, and something self-evidently true about the truth.' (p. 70)

....

3. Standing firm in the faith (3:10–15a)

1 What does Paul mean when he says that Timothy knows about him? Why is this important? How does it relate to the first half of the chapter?

2 How would you answer someone who suggested that Paul is being rather conceited in drawing attention to his virtues in verses 10–11?

3 What 'good (though not infallible) general tests of people's sincerity, and even of the truth or error of their systems' (p. 73) are highlighted here? How do these apply to you?

4 Why is persecution 'inevitable' (p. 75)? In what ways do you experience this?

5 Why might Timothy need to be told to 'continue' (verse 14) in what he has learned and firmly believed?

6 What reasons does Paul give for Timothy to do this?

7 How can we tell whether a new way of going about things is good or bad?

4. The origin and purpose of Scripture (3:15b–17)

1 What 'two central truths' (pp. 78f.) about the Bible does Paul set out here?

2 How would you answer someone who claimed that only certain parts of the Bible were inspired by God?

3 How do we know what Paul means by 'all Scripture' (verse 16)?

4 In what ways is Scripture 'useful' (p. 79)? What recent examples of this have you seen in your own life?

5 'Scripture is the chief means which God employs to bring *the servant of God* to maturity' (p. 80). How does this work out in practice for you?

4. The charge to preach the gospel (pp. 82–102)

1. The nature of the charge (4:2)

1 What would Timothy have understood by the instruction to 'preach the word' (p. 83)?

2 What does Paul say about the sort of preaching he wants Timothy to undertake? How does what he says apply to you?

2. The basis of the charge (4:1, 3–8)

1 What incentives does Paul give to encourage Timothy? How are these relevant for us today?

2 What does it mean to have 'itching ears' (verse 3)? What is surprising about the way in which Timothy is to respond to this situation?

....

'The harder the times and the deafer the people, the clearer and more persuasive our proclamation must be.' (p. 88)

....

3 What is significant about the way Paul describes his own ministry?

4 Are you looking forward to the return of Christ? Why? What lies behind Paul's enthusiasm for this event?

3. An illustration of the charge (4:9–22)

1 What are the factors which have contributed to Paul's sense of isolation?

2 What human needs does Paul reveal here?

3 How does Paul's experience relate to what he has been asking Timothy to do?

4 'In all our Christian life and service we should embrace no other way of thinking than this' (p. 102). To what is John Stott referring? How true is this of your outlook on life?

The Bible Speaks Today:
Old Testament series

The Message of Genesis 1 – 11
The dawn of creation
David Atkinson

The Message of Genesis 12 – 50
From Abraham to Joseph
Joyce G. Baldwin

The Message of Exodus
The days of our pilgrimage
Alec Motyer

The Message of Leviticus
Free to be holy
Derek Tidball

The Message of Numbers
Journey to the promised land
Raymond Brown

The Message of Deuteronomy
Not by bread alone
Raymond Brown

The Message of Joshua
Promise and people
David G. Firth

The Message of Judges
Grace abounding
Michael Wilcock

The Message of Ruth
The wings of refuge
David Atkinson

The Message of Samuel
Personalities, potential, politics and power
Mary J. Evans

The Message of Kings
God is present
John W. Olley

The Message of Chronicles
One church, one faith, one Lord
Michael Wilcock

The Message of Ezra and Haggai
Building for God
Robert Fyall

The Message of Nehemiah
God's servant in a time of change
Raymond Brown

The Message of Esther
God present but unseen
David G. Firth

The Message of Job
Suffering and grace
David Atkinson

The Bible Speaks Today:
New Testament series

The Message of Matthew
The kingdom of heaven
Michael Green

The Message of Mark
The mystery of faith
Donald English

The Message of Luke
The Saviour of the world
Michael Wilcock

The Message of John
Here is your King!
Bruce Milne

**The Message of the Sermon
on the Mount (Matthew 5 – 7)**
Christian counter-culture
John Stott

The Message of Acts
To the ends of the earth
John Stott

The Message of Romans
God's good news for the world
John Stott

The Message of 1 Corinthians
Life in the local church
David Prior

The Message of 2 Corinthians
Power in weakness
Paul Barnett

The Message of Galatians
Only one way
John Stott

The Message of Ephesians
God's new society
John Stott

The Message of Philippians
Jesus our joy
Alec Motyer

**The Message of Colossians and
Philemon**
Fullness and freedom
Dick Lucas

**The Message of
1 and 2 Thessalonians**
Preparing for the coming King
John Stott

The Bible Speaks Today: Bible Themes series

The Message of the Living God
His glory, his people, his world
Peter Lewis

The Message of the Resurrection
Christ is risen!
Paul Beasley-Murray

The Message of the Cross
Wisdom unsearchable, love indestructible
Derek Tidball

The Message of Salvation
By God's grace, for God's glory
Philip Graham Ryken

The Message of Creation
Encountering the Lord of the universe
David Wilkinson

The Message of Heaven and Hell
Grace and destiny
Bruce Milne

The Message of Mission
The glory of Christ in all time and space
Howard Peskett and Vinoth Ramachandra

The Message of Prayer
Approaching the throne of grace
Tim Chester

The Message of the Trinity
Life in God
Brian Edgar

The Message of Evil and Suffering
Light into darkness
Peter Hicks

The Message of the Holy Spirit
The Spirit of encounter
Keith Warrington

The Message of Holiness
Restoring God's masterpiece
Derek Tidball

The Message of Sonship
At home in God's household
Trevor Burke

The Message of the Word of God
The glory of God made known
Tim Meadowcroft

The Message of Women
Creation, grace and gender
Derek and Dianne Tidball

The Message of the Church
Assemble the people before me
Chris Green

The Message of the Person of Christ
The Word made flesh
Robert Letham

The Message of Worship
Celebrating the glory of God in the whole of life
John Risbridger

The Message of Spiritual Warfare
The Lord is a warrior; the Lord is his name
Keith Ferdinando

The Message of Discipleship
Authentic followers of Jesus in today's world
Peter Morden

The Message of Love
The only thing that counts
Patrick Mitchel

The Message of Wisdom
Learning and living the way of the Lord
Daniel J. Estes

Printed and bound by CPI Group (UK) Ltd, Croydon, CR0 4YY

13/03/2025

01833318-0008